Extraordinary Praise ~

# MENSPIRATION

There is a highly visible and much needed "Me Too" movement where women are naming their pain, speaking their voices, and charting a course to an empowered future. We must be very careful that we do not minimize or compromise this movement, but as women claim the gift of their authentic being, they should not have to deal with dead men. We need a movement that transforms deceived and destructive men who practice death in a hierarchy of value where men are superior and women and children are victims.

Ronald Thornhill provides the "Menspiration" that can guide men to alter presently accepted thoughts and behaviors as they discover their true identity, value, and promise. This book is written by a man to motivate and inspire men, but its suggestive counsel can provide signposts leading to a new humanity and a new earth.

—**John W. Kinney**
Professor of Theology
School of Theology at Virginia Union University

*Menspiration* is a compelling guide of how men should equip themselves mentally and spiritually to confront life's daily struggles and persistent pressures. The illustrations used in this book demonstrate how we can use internal and external factors to elevate our God-given gifts to make us greater men and the world around us a better place. *Menspiration* is also a reference of how we can balance our spiritual and physical beings with our moral consciousness. It's a must read!

—**Bryant Stith**
Former National Basketball Association Player

*Menspiration* is not only a vital asset for men but for anyone, male or female who have the deep desire and conviction to move from painful pits to divine destiny. Utilizing his own personal experiences, Dr. Ronald Thornhill courageously takes us on an inspirational journey that will motivate us all.

**—Dr. Deborah M. Martin**
Pastor, Real Life Ministries

# MEN
## SPIRATION

# MEN SPIRATION

**MOTIVATING & INSPIRING MEN TO CONQUER LIFE'S MOUNTAINS**

## DR. RONALD K. THORNHILL SR.

COOKE HOUSE
PUBLISHING
WINSTON SALEM

**MENSPIRATION: MOTIVATING & INSPIRING MEN TO CONQUER LIFE'S MOUNTAINS**

Copyright © 2018 – Ronald K. Thornhill

All rights reserved. This book is protected by the copyright laws of the United States of America. This book may not be copied or reprinted for commercial gain or profit. The use of quotations or occasional page copying for personal or group study is permitted and encouraged. Permission will be granted upon request.

Unless otherwise identified, Scripture quotations are from the King James Version. Copyright © 1982 by Thomas Nelson, Inc. Used by permission. All rights reserved.

Scripture quotations marked (NLT) are taken from the Holy Bible, New Living Translation, copyright © 1996. Used by permission of Tyndale House Publishers, Inc., Wheaton, IL 60189 USA. All rights reserved.

Soft cover ISBN: 978-0-9988313-6-7
E-Book ISBN: 978-0-0088313-7-4

Library of Congress Cataloging-in-Publication Data is available upon request

Cooke House Publishing
(a division of Cooke Consulting & Creations, LLC)
Winston-Salem, NC
publishing@cookecc.org

This book and all Cooke House Publishing books are available at bookstores and distributors worldwide.

Printed in the United States of America.- First Edition

*To Trice, my wife, my greatest supporter
in every venture and all that I have ever sought out to do.
In tough times and in good times, you have epitomized
those words and what it really means for better or for worse.
Thanks for sticking with me and loving me even when I did not
love myself. Love you much.*

*To my children, Ashley and Ronald and even my grandson Josh,
I love you all so much for being all you can be and trusting the
process even when the process sometimes did not make sense or
got cloudy along the way.*

*Finally, to my grandmother, the one
woman who perhaps help chart my course to where I am
and who I am today. Love you, Grandma.*

# CONTENTS

FOREWORD — 11

INTRODUCTION — 13
**Menspiration**
*Mending and Blending Inspiration and Motivation to Change the Game*

CHAPTER 1 — 17
**Meeting the Challenge as Men - the "M" in Menspiration**
*So, Who Do I Follow to Get the True Picture?*

CHAPTER 2 — 33
**Expecting More with Less - The "E" in Menspiration**
*A Model for Training Before Our Reigning*

CHAPTER 3 — 32
**Narrative as Men - The "N" in Menspiration**
*Writing Our Own Story*

CHAPTER 4 — 49
**Shifting the Paradigm - The "S" in Menspiration**
*Willing to Do the Difficult Things*

CHAPTER 5 — 57
**Pursuing Our Passion - The "P" in Menspiration**
*So What You Messed Up*

CHAPTER 6 — 65
**Inspiration versus Frustration - The "I" in Menspiration**
*A New Perspective on Getting It Done*

### Chapter 7 — 75
**Recovery Process - The "R" in Menspiration**
*Maintaining Your Healing*

### Chapter 8 — 87
**Accepting Who We Are - The "A" in Menspiration**
*Stop Trying to Be Like Mike*

### Chapter 9 — 93
**Taking Risks - The "T" in Menspiration**
*It's Part of the Process*

### Chapter 10 — 101
**Igniting the Fire - The "I" in Menspiration**
*You Were Made in His Image, So Go For It*

### Chapter 11 — 109
**Owning Your Destiny - The "O" in Menspiration**
*Don't Let No One Hijack Your Destiny*

### Chapter 12 — 119
**Never say Never - The "N" in Menspiration**
*Who Knows, This May Be Your Time*

### A Final Word — 126
**Menspiration - Mending and Blending a New Way of Life**

*Endnotes* — 129
*About the Author* — 130

# FOREWORD

At a young age, Ronald Thornhill had a great ability to communicate his message of perseverance, while emphasizing the importance of teamwork. His commitment to hard work and his determination to stay a part of a team tells a very inspirational story that all people should have a chance to hear. Menspiration shares with all of us his heartfelt, grace-saturated story that does not sugar-coat reality; instead he conveys the pain and heartache, the disappointment of sacrifice, and ultimately the joy of fulfillment in being a part of something larger than self—the enduring perspective of a teammate. I watched him over the years wear the various hats of father, pastor, coach, and school administrator so well. At times I wondered how he was able to do it, but having coached him and witnessed him lead our team as a star point guard, eventually it was no surprise to me. Dr. Thornhill's message resonates with folks as old as 7 x 7, and as young as 7.

After sixty continual years of either playing on a team, coaching a team, or watching team-members participate, I can safely say there are many SERMONS in my eyes, ears, and mind! The sermon Ronald Thornhill continues to "preach" could be entitled, "STAY THE COURSE!" As an athlete, pastor, teacher, coach, neighbor, leader, and friend, I heard, saw, and listened to him for the last 44 years of our relationship that same on-course life sermon. His core values seldom needed adjustment, therefore assessments of what was and what is, remained constant. People need to be appreciated for who they are now. Looking at a person is far different from just seeing them . . . when they have been nurtured! Athlete, pastor, teacher, coach, neighbor, leader, friend—Ronald Thornhill NURTURED all of us WELL!

CONGRATULATIONS My Role Model!

—George B. Lancaster Jr.
Legendary high school coach and educator for over 50 years

# INTRODUCTION
*Mending and Blending Inspiration and Motivation to Change the Game*

Have you ever been inspired to do something after hearing a great speech or after reading a book that you just could not put down, only to have your inspiration or mojo shattered because as time passed, you ended up doing nothing with what you heard or read? It was not that you lost your inspiration or that you did not want to do anything, but time simply crept in along with so many other things. However, at the end of the day, you were still at square one. Well, join the bandwagon of many of us—particularly men—as we take a journey from motivation and inspiration, to finding our menspiration, something that was lost when we fell in the Garden of Eden. It is my belief that motivation is inward and can only come from within, while inspiration is outward and for the most part can come from anyone. On the other hand, menspiration is a combination of both— the mending and blending of experiences, encounters, and explorations to help us become all that we can be as men.

Moreover, *Menspiration* will take you on a journey of motivational and inspirational stories as told from the perspective of a father, pastor, coach, and educator. While the stories are not intended to be exhaustive, they will give you a picture of the struggles we all face as men and some workable solutions.

Amazingly, what sometimes seem to be the least resistant and less painful route to success is not always the best route. Recently, I had arthroscopic knee surgery due to a torn meniscus. Prior to the surgery, the doctor had given me several options I could have taken instead of surgery. First, I could have received a cortisone shot to reduce the pain that would have lasted approximately six months to one year. Secondly, I could undergo physical therapy to see if that would ease the pain. Finally, I could simply have knee surgery to repair the torn meniscus and remove the fragments around my knee.

---

*... what sometimes seem to be the least resistant and less painful route to success is not always the best route.*

---

While it took me almost six months to decide to have the surgery, it only took one day after the surgery to realize I made the right decision. Sometimes we prefer a cortisone shot for our problems, not realizing that it only masks the real issue. It will give you temporary relief, but just like my meniscus, there are situations in your life that are still torn, and sooner or later other (possibly more severe) problems will surface and you are back where you started. Physical therapy is great for now, but unless we continue the therapy every day, the meniscus and your struggles will eventually tighten up again making it difficult to deal with each day.

As men, sometimes we receive great words from other men at conferences or some other men's event and we are inspired when we go back home. Unfortunately, it's like the cortisone shot; it only lasts for a short while, and soon we are back to limping on that same leg or struggling to find another way to cope with the pain.

To some the thought of surgery conjures up many emotions. For me, it wasn't just the pain, but all that comes along with surgery, such as the anesthesia, the incisions that had to be made, and yes, I struggled with the thought of whether I would wake up from being out for an hour. While all of this was very real to me, here is the truth moment: of all the preconceived notions I had about the surgery, nothing compared to the pain I experienced daily at work. No one could see it, but there were days I could barely walk because my knee would tighten and lock up on me because of the tear. It was a battle some days to walk from my car to the office building.

Even though I was inspired by others who had the surgery and motivated by reading several articles related to arthroscopic knee surgery, I still had some inner fears because of the death of a close friend who developed blood clots from a knee surgery. Although I would like to think that my faith was greater than my fears, the truth of the matter was that I had to decide whether I wanted to live with constant pain or have the surgery.

Sometimes we are faced with similar situations, deciding whether to live with the constant pain of what our fathers did or did not do. In other cases, some of us did not have a father at all to model after or turn to when we needed critical answers for life. With my torn meniscus, those tears were not visible, but they were affecting my daily life. Similarly, some of you may have struggles or problems that are underneath the surface but are eating away at the fabric of your being, and surgery (tearing and cutting away what's causing the pain and repairing what remains) may be your last but best option. Therefore, as we journey together to take a closer look at what's really been eating at us for years, let's be willing to at least confront the issue, deal with it from an arthroscopic or closer perspective to address the problem, and then allow the recovery process to take its true course in our lives.

This book will serve as a blueprint as to how to navigate through life's toughest battles, especially when you come to those places in life where you have never been, and the GPS cannot get you further, as it simply keeps recalculating without providing further instruction. There are no free passes through life, no get out of jail free cards, nor is there any pie in the sky when we go bye and bye. It's all about real life, with real issues, and a real God who can help us through real problems.

After all, timing is everything. I don't believe you just happened to pick up this book, nor do I believe I just happened to be writing it. There is always a master plan behind all that we do and experience in life. The key, however, is when the time is right, we must seize the opportunity because when it passes, you cannot recover it.

My hope is that you don't view this book as another cortisone shot to make us feel better as men, or physical therapy for the daily struggles we face in life, but rather a serious conversation on the prospects of an arthroscopic surgical approach to help correct some existing "tears" in our lives.

## Chapter 1
# Meeting the Challenges as Men
*So, Who Do I Follow to Get the True Picture?*

Being raised in the city of Richmond, VA, particularly in the sixties and seventies, it was not hard finding a job if you really wanted to work. Now I must qualify that statement: as a teenager, the available jobs included cutting grass, shining shoes, raking leaves, and shoveling snow. The question was simply did you really want to work? In my case, I loved to dress well, and I loved the latest styles, so I worked.

Growing up, my father was my model and my example as a provider. Although he never spent the time I wish he could have spent with me due to his work schedule, he always made sure I had what I needed. However, on one occasion when I was a senior in high school and was playing my last basketball game, my father showed up to this game still wearing the bowtie and blazer he had worn to work. He came straight from work to support me. This memory stands out in my mind the most, not because it was my last game as a senior, but because it was the only game my father ever attended. To see him at the final game of my high school career didn't make up for four years of me looking in the stands wondering if he would ever show up, so his presence that night startled me. At that time, I did not understand why he only attended that one game. It was later that I realized having three brothers and two sisters somebody had to make sure we had food on the table.

Later in life, the one thing that I learned from my father was his work ethic. There was never a time that I can recall when he did not work. Even when he got injured in a domestic incident and could not drive, he still caught the bus to work. I remember on another occasion when I was a freshman in high school, he missed my school registration because he had to work overtime. He is now well in his eighties and he still works three to four days a week. Another thing I remember about my time with my father is that he did take my brothers and I fishing. This is why I love fishing today. This proved to be invaluable because it is the one thing that brings my son and I together today. Each year we plan a fishing trip together with a few other men as a time to get away and spend with one another just to have fun.

Let's pause for a moment. I think we spend more time working to build a future for our family, but less time building better relationships at home. For example, my father was a great provider, but we never really had the kind of relationship where we would talk about school, work, sports, or anything for that matter. I can remember when I was about eight years old going through my father's desk drawer and finding a big sock filled with quarters, dimes, and nickels. I'm sure it was over two hundred dollars in change. When I asked him about giving me a few dollars, he quickly reminded me that he was saving it for my future. In retrospect, I wish he would have spent the money on a fishing rod or bicycle and taught me how to ride a bike. Looking back through the telescope of time, I realize now that no future earnings can replace the time lost with your parents when growing up.

I'm not suggesting that securing a financial future is not important, but without a family to spend that future with is meaningless. I appreciate not having to want for anything when growing up, but it still would have been nice to see my father at some of our school events. I don't recall too many events that he attended with any of my siblings. I'm sure he probably had one thing in mind—make that money—especially with six children and a wife to feed. Although at times it's hard to choose between making extra money for the sake of your family or spending time with the family, balance is the key to it all. Perhaps if my father would have chosen to attend at least one event per month for me or one of my siblings, it might have worked. However, I do remember coming home one Friday when I was away in college and my father and I attended a football game of my youngest brother. This conceivably was one of the coolest times I ever shared with my father. It was his first game he ever attended, and my brother scored several touchdowns. After my brother scored, my father leaned over to me and said, "I did not know he was that good." I wanted to say, *Dad if you had taken the time to come to see him play earlier, you would have known.*

Many times, we struggle with insecurity issues because we never took the time to build a proper relationship with those whom we love. In my father's case, I believe he was never secure in building a relationship with those he loved because he never had a relationship with his father. As a result, he simply worked all the time to cover up his issues, as many of us tend to do. Even today when we attend family functions, my father never stays more than an hour before he's ready to go home. When we don't build proper relationships, we tend to feel that we have to earn our way or work our way to getting others to accept us. I believe this has a lot to do with why my father worked so much trying to make life better for us, but also covering up deficiencies in his life.

We all can fall into the same pattern if we don't recognize the symptoms and then be willing to do something about it. I have not always been the best in that department and will be the first to admit that I needed help. Early in my marriage I worked two jobs thinking that it would help us to get ahead, especially since I had just had my second child, but it still did not make up for time loss. I soon recognized that I had fallen into the same pattern as my father, always working but never spending time with my family. I guess I was more like my father than I realized.

It was not until I attended church one Sunday and the minister asked me when did I plan to stop following my plan and start following God's plan. It bothered me so much that I went home and studied the text from which the minister preached: "For God so loved the world. . ."(John 3:16). After reading this scripture, I got a better understanding of what a father is supposed to do at home and at work. Although I had grown up in church, I never had anyone to explain that particular scripture to me.

After much study, I concluded that our biological fathers are great men, but they are flawed at best. The only perfect example is our heavenly Father. He modeled the message of giving your best when you love something the most. This was critical because as men we are constantly trying to follow or model our lives after someone we admire, even if it's our earthly fathers. However, when they mess up or don't live up to our expectations, we look for others to follow. Although now it is clear to me that the Lord is the one to follow, we must always remember to trust the process that our heavenly Father laid out for us through his son Jesus. This process would include sacrificing those things that we love and mean the most to us with the hope of a greater return and reward in the future. Growing up with five siblings, it was hard to trust the process, but as time would progress, the Lord sent a coach, a principal, and a pastor who would help me through the process.

### The Struggle is Real

Sometimes as children we do not see the struggles and challenges our parents face to provide for us, but at the end of the day we are thankful that we survived. So often we make the mistake in saying we are going to raise our children differently, only to find out that we are more like our parents than we realize. For example, as much as I would like to think I did it "my way" as Frank Sinatra would say, I am sure my dad would probably laugh if he heard some of the same expressions I said to my children that he said to us.

It has been said that a picture is worth a thousand words. Well, the picture that my father painted as a provider, a husband, and as a mentor, is similar to who I am today. I find myself doing and saying some of the same things to my children, wife, and even my students at school. In some cases, he did everything by the book: he worked, took care of my mother, and always gave us some of the best gifts for Christmas, especially money. On the other hand, he could use a few lessons on how to spend quality time with his family, how to balance work with pleasure, and simply how to have fun. One of the most difficult things for me and my brothers to deal with was never seeing our father at many, if any, of our games. Because we all played so many sports, even if he had showed up at some of the games it would have been great. Even though we have an obligation to support our families financially, we must remember to support them in other ways as well, particularly as it relates to our physical presence at events. It's not always easy to choose one over the other, but being intentional by showing up makes all the difference in the world.

I might have been a good provider for my family; however, on the other hand, I am not so proud of the picture

I painted as a husband and father by not showing emotions and affection toward my family. No, I wasn't the worst, but there are a lot of areas where I could have done better. I am not suggesting or making excuses for my failures, but looking at my father as a role model in certain areas was sketchy at best. He was a great provider, but I never witnessed him showing any affection or emotions toward my mother or any of my siblings.

With that said, it's amazing how much is caught from our parents than taught. In other words, I learned what to do as well as what not to do, simply by watching my parents. Even at times when it was not intentional, I found myself modeling or doing some of the same things they did when I was a child. It's important to note that as parents we are constantly being watched by our children. Therefore, what we do, say, and how we respond, is like a video recording. Everything that was recorded, is played back later in life. Though my parents never divorced, I knew they had their challenges. Beyond that, the image my father portrayed to me would soon be the one I portrayed to my son. I only wonder how this ongoing picture would frame the course and context for the future my son will paint for his family. So, my dilemma was who do I follow to get the true picture of how I should respond as a husband, father, and mentor to my son and daughter.

### The Church is Not Always the Answer

This may be a hard pill to swallow, and I do not mean it in a disrespectful manner, but the church is not always the answer. I thought it was, but I was rudely mistaken. The church was just as dysfunctional as my family, and by this I mean not normal. First, let me clarify some things. I am a pastor and by no means am I suggesting that all churches are dysfunctional. In my case, I grew up in the Pentecostal Church and the standards were much stricter than others. We believed that you could not go to the movies, play sports, go swimming, or anything that was considered *worldly*. Ladies could not wear pants or earrings and their dresses had to be worn below the knees. Although this was a part of the church government, I, like others, just adhered to it. However, some of us who loved sports and other outdoor activities played anyway.

Because my grandmother essentially raised me, and she was Pentecostal, it was not optional for me. What I found to be dysfunctional was not necessarily the dress but the attitude of leadership. They espoused to the "do as I say and not as I do" mentality. On one occasion, I encountered a mother struggling with trying to buy food for her family. When I approached the church leadership with the mother, they told her they could not help because she was not saved and needed to get her life together. At the time, the woman had no place to go and had no money to feed her children. Even though I knew we had a missionary fund and money to help the mother, the church still refused to help. I later found out that the woman was a former member of the church and the leadership refused to help because she left the church. The sad commentary was that the lady who was in need was a relative of another member of the church but because she was not liked by many, nothing was done for her. This incident was one of many that took place at the church I attended, and it left me wondering is this how we all operate.

As I got older and visited other churches, I realized that all churches are not the same. I'm also proud to say I do not feel the same as I felt earlier about church. The church I joined later helped me to see things a little differently. Although they helped people who were in need such as the poor and others who had been released from prison, their major emphasis was not on a hand out, but a hand up. They focused more on providing training to those individuals who experienced problems with homelessness and recovery from alcohol and drugs, rather than just giving them money for a particular need. There are dysfunctional churches as well as dysfunctional families who operate from a different set of norms, but we must all strive to live out the golden rule of do unto others as you would have them to do unto you.

As a church, it's a part of our covenant to help those who are less fortunate. In some ways, the church perpetuates a dysfunctional attitude when we only help those who are a part of our immediate circle instead of helping *all* those who are in need. The church tells us to pray about our challenges but never provides any real strategies or plan of action to assist families through their challenges. I now believe that we can change the dysfunctional attitude by fulfilling the great commission as found in Matthew 28:19—"Go ye therefore and teach all nations . . ." The operative word is *teach*. When individuals are taught, they can then *do*. This I believe is the key to dispelling a dysfunctional attitude in the church.

Even though I grew up in the church and my grandmother was the assistant pastor of that church, we had our challenges as well. I remember one incident where the Sunday school teacher said something to me, and I cried the entire time I was in church. When my grandmother found out what happened, she approached the Sunday school teacher and gave her a few choice words. Because the Sunday school teacher was the sister of the pastor, the incident went on for several months with me being in the middle. The situation was finally resolved, and I discovered that my grandmother was a force in the church, especially when it came to her grandchildren. This was a time when my siblings and I learned who the real boss was in our family. It was evident by the way she handled the Sunday school teacher. In addition, I soon discovered that my grandfather, who was a deacon in the church, also respected my grandmother. In fact, he never went against her concerning matters of the church.

### The Lasting Influence of a Grandmother
Perhaps this is why my grandmother's influence is highly visible in my life today. I never would have met or married my

wife had I not gone to a convention that my grandmother took me to every year as a child. I pastor a church in the town of Lawrenceville, Virginia because my grandmother encouraged me to go to college in that town. I pursued my master's and doctorate degree because my grandmother told me that education was the bridge to success. At one point while I was in college, I moved in with my grandmother because I was struggling to maintain my grades at school. While I could go on and on about the influence that my grandmother had in my life, I will conclude simply by saying we all are sketches and portraits of our parents and grandparents.

When I look at my life today as a school administrator, pastor, community leader, and social activist, I can honestly say I was framed by what my grandmother instilled in me at an early age. Sometimes, for better or worse, we might not like how we were framed or what we look like to others, but we were all framed by someone. The beauty, however, is that the master artist, God himself, is still sketching our lives, and if the canvas of our heart is pliable, it will be worth the journey in following him. He sees and knows things about us that we don't know. Furthermore, the prophet Jeremiah states, "For I know the plans I have for you, declares the Lord, plans to prosper you and not to harm you, plans to give you hope and a future" (Jeremiah 29:11). This statement alone assures us of who we should follow. Sometimes our natural parents desire the best for us, but they don't know the plans for our future or what detours we may encounter. For the most part, we don't know what tomorrow holds, but according to Jeremiah 29:11, we know who holds tomorrow.

### The Potter is Still Shaping the Vessel

I was reminded of a similar picture when the Lord told the prophet Jeremiah (Jer. 18:1-11) to go down to the potter's house to get a picture of the present state of the nation. The picture that Jeremiah framed was that of a damaged vessel of clay. To make matters worse, the vessel was damaged while still in the hands of the potter. To show us what the Lord can do when we appear to be *damaged goods*, the potter crushed the lump of clay and started over again. Sometimes we have to be crushed and made over again to become the vessels that the Lord intended for our lives. We may have been following the wrong person or the wrong influence until we are taken down to the potter's house to get a better picture of who to follow.

In this illustration of the potter's house we see the preparation of clay, the molding of clay, the strengthening of clay, and the purpose of clay. Interestingly, the only clay that makes it to the wheel is the clay that has already been softened by the potter and the clay that has the potential to be a great vessel. After seeing what the potter was able to do, the Lord raised a rhetorical question: "Can I not do to you what the potter has done with his clay?" (Jeremiah 18:6). The same can be said of us, even after all the mistakes we made following others. We, too, can be made over again if we choose to follow the Lord. Sometimes it may be a bad marriage, a bad childhood, or a poor relationship with our fathers, but the Lord reminded Jeremiah that it did not have to stay that way. In other words, he could change it all if the vessel was willing to be made over again.

We all have been a part of some sort of tragedy in our lives, from the death of a loved one, the divorce of parents, the loss of a job, or some other incident that rips our hearts out. However, the key to change is the acknowledgement that there are some "tears" in our lives and the willingness to endure surgery to correct the issue. Moreover, the fact that the potter is still shaping the vessel, assures us that we can survive any "tear" or tragedy in our lives when we are willing to be made over again.

In the spiritual sense, correcting the tear has more to do with the heart than anything else. In the process of being made over again, our hearts have to be conditioned to forgive if we are ever going to be made over. Forgiveness is akin to unclogging an artery that's been blocked by something or someone who hurt, disappointed, or failed us. When we forgive those who hurt us, we become new vessels in the hand of the potter and can love again. This is paramount because one of the major indicators that we are followers of Jesus has to do with our love for one another (John 13:35). So regardless of how severe the "tear" might be in our lives, especially as it relates to our heart, it can be corrected because we have the best heart specialist available, Jesus Christ. When I made the decision to have knee surgery, I asked the doctor would I be 100 percent after the surgery and he said, "No, probably 70 percent." But 70 percent was much better than the zero percent I was feeling at the time. As men, sometimes we want to get off the potter's wheel because we are only functioning at 70 percent. However, if we just stay on the wheel, we will eventually get to 100 percent because he is reshaping us every day of our lives.

### How are We Framing Our Picture?

As a result of my father being absent at all of my games except one, I vowed to be at all my son's and daughter's games throughout their careers. This would include middle school, high school, and college. While this was the picture that framed how I would raise my children, it only created a "tear" in my life that caused me to develop a limp that got worse over time. In my efforts to paint a different picture from my father regarding my son, I overlooked some other areas that would prove to be detrimental in the future. Ironically, one of the same struggles my father had in his life my son struggled with it as well.

Growing up, I watched my father drink as a way of coping with the stress from working long hours. He would be considered by some as a functional alcoholic because he only drank when he got home. He would never drink in front of me or my siblings, but we all knew when he had been drinking. Eventually over a period of time, I could tell the effects of my father's drinking because of the abusive treatment towards my mother. While many of us can recount the horror stories after watching parents who were functional alcoholics, abusive, or just never there, it does not have to frame how we raise our children today. If we are ever going to break this generational cycle, we must be intentional by confronting and talking about it openly with our children and those we love.

I mentioned earlier that there was a tear in my son's life and it was alcohol as well. This tear got worse before it got better. One of the most frustrating things for me was to see him lose the edge he had as an outstanding basketball player. His senior year in high school he was the state player of the year. His first two years in college he led the conference in three-point field goals made. In those same two years, he led his team to consecutive conference championships. His third year, I noticed a difference in his play and his attitude. It was because of his drinking. I did not realize it was bad until I received a call from the coach informing me that my son was arrested for driving under the influence. I thought going to Charlotte, NC where he resided and giving him a stern talk would handle the situation, but it got worse. Not long after that, he got stopped again for driving under the influence, and this time his license was suspended. At this point, I was really upset and threatened to take his car and bring it back to Virginia. But I did not take the car, and he got stopped again for driving on a suspended license. As a result, he spent thirty days incarcerated on the weekends and his license was revoked for five years.

While this was a tough pill for my son to swallow, the fact that he is still dealing with the effects of it today is gut wrenching. On every job application he fills out, he must list those offenses. To add insult to injury, he was denied several good jobs due to his arrest record for drinking. As painful as it is for me to share his story, my hope is that other fathers will do what I failed to do. Instead of showing some tough love and taking the car, I continued to hope it would get better. All the signs were there that my son had a problem with drinking, but I failed to pay closer attention because I was always busy.

  When my son was younger and played AAU basketball, my wife, daughter, and I would travel all over the country to support him. I wanted to make sure I was there for him unlike my father was for me. It was no secret that this was intentional, but over time, I realized that there were some "emotional tears" developing that needed to be corrected. In other words, I was spending time at games, but not spending time with him personally. When my son was older, he told me it would upset him to no end when we were out playing together, and I would receive a call from someone at church. Those calls weren't just a few minutes, sometimes they lasted an hour or longer. Because this happened so often, my son just said he did not want to play with me anymore. I thought it was because he was busy or tired, but I later found out it was due to the calls and me making the church a priority over him.

  Ironically, I was at all my son's games from middle school to college, but still not in his life as a father. The times that he perhaps needed me the most, I was helping someone else, all in the name of the church. I am not suggesting that I was derelict in my duties as a father, but I was so busy helping others that I did not take care of home. Sometimes we overcompensate as fathers by trying to do and give our sons what we did not get, only to end up still missing the mark in some other area of their lives. This reminds me of a skilled surgeon who travels all over the world to perform major heart transplants, but never has the time to perform minor surgery, such as a damaged artery, on his own son.

**TRUTH MOMENT**

The greatest challenge and perhaps a major regret for me in trying to find out who to follow was overlooking the one who was right there all along. Although my father was missing in action at all of my games during the time I was growing up, his impact at home and in other areas helped to make me the man and the father I am today. At home, he always expressed to my brothers and me the importance of a strong work ethic. He helped me get my first job as a waiter even though I was only fourteen at the time. He took the time to show me how to tie a necktie. Now this may seem like a small thing, but to see the number of young men in school today who cannot tie a necktie helps me to appreciate the little things my father taught me. At that time, we did not have YouTube® to teach us, but I'm glad we did not because there is nothing like a personal touch.

Amazingly, something as small as watching how patient my father was in teaching me, helped to shape the teacher in me. What I did see, relative to his work ethic and taking care of home, perhaps outweighed what I did not see from an emotional side. This is by no means an excuse or bailout for him not showing any affection toward us while growing up, but now I know he could only do what was modeled in front of him. In his case, there was no model because he never met his father.

Sadly, in my attempt to do things so differently from him with my son, I created a different "tear" in my son's life. It is a "tear" that would not show up immediately, but over a period of time, and would create a limp in his life. I was not there for my son when he needed me the most and it resulted in him drinking as a way to ease the pain. Although I fell short when it came to be there for my son, teaching him to follow Jesus was the next best thing that I could do for him.
I have come to the realization to leave the surgical work up to the master surgeon. He created us, knows us better than we

know ourselves, and above all, makes the necessary adjustments in our lives without damaging the "tendons," the part that connects us to others who are vital to our well-being. Even with all our shortcomings as natural fathers we have hope in knowing that we can look to our heavenly Father who can show us a more excellent way to live out our true purpose as fathers.

## Chapter 2
# Expecting More with Less
*A Model of Training Before Our Reigning*

Prior to my surgery, I read a lot of material about arthroscopic knee surgery. Unfortunately, the more I read, the less I was inclined to proceed with the surgery. My problem was that I focused more on the risks instead of the benefits. The risks included bleeding, infection, blood clots, stiffness or ongoing pain in the joints, damage to the cartilage, damage to the blood vessels and nerves, and other risks as outlined by the doctor. So, as you can see, I could have benefited more with less knowledge. This is not to suggest that we should enter anything, let alone surgery, without conducting research and becoming better informed about major decisions. However, sometimes more is not always better, especially when we focus on the negatives rather than the positives.

In my case, the benefits were that arthroscopic surgery was very safe and I would feel much better after the surgery. The challenge, as in any case, would be if I could see the benefits rather than allow the risks to cloud my judgment. As men we are sometimes charged with making those tough decisions regarding our family, our job, and maybe even church. The risks of what others may say, how many times we messed up in the past, or how we may be following in the same pattern as our fathers, should never stop us from doing what others are afraid to do. The less we listen to the doubters, the naysayers, and the peanut gallery, the more we can accomplish with the help of God. The more I examined the process of arthroscopic knee surgery, the more I realized it was just "training for my reigning."

Yes, I did say reigning, and yes, men, we are all kings in our own dominion, but we must learn the art of protecting our dominion—those things that have been entrusted to us by our heavenly Father. For example, we protect our dominion by following the words of King Solomon: "Train up a child in the way he should go: and when he is old, he will not depart from it" (Proverbs 22:6). I know we cannot protect our children from everything, but by training them we can at least put them in a position to make quality decisions later in life. Furthermore, the decisions we make now can affect us for the rest of our life. Training may not always take place at home or familiar surroundings, but it may take place on the football field, basketball court, or even the baseball diamond. The key to the training process is that it involves the teaching of a particular skill or type of behavior through practice and instruction over a period of time.

Legendary college football coach Nick Saban, who just recently won his sixth national championship, epitomizes the training before the reigning process. Prior to him winning his first national championship, he coached five college football teams, two professional football teams, and was fired from one college team. All of this took place over a span of 37 years. Even though this was a challenging process going from team to team, it was worth the struggle since now many consider him to be the greatest college football coach ever. Amazingly, his training did not stop with the young men he coached, but it also laid the foundation for his assistant coaches to become head coaches. Our training does not stop with the sweat and tears we experience along the way, but it paves the way for us becoming the future leaders we are today. Eight of Saban's assistant coaches are now head coaches of major college programs. As men, we must always remember that whatever we experience during one chapter of our life is simply preparation for what we may encounter in another chapter. In Saban's book *How Good Do You Want to Be*, he was asked by news reporters how did he handle the rigors of coaching along with the struggles of going from team to team earlier in his career. He responded, "There are two pains in life: the pain of discipline and the pain of disappointment. If you can handle the pain of discipline, then you'll never have to deal with the pain of disappointment."[1] The late Vince Lombardi, coach of the Green Bay Packers, summed it up best: "Football is a great deal like life in that it teaches us that work, sacrifice, perseverance, competitive drive, selflessness, and respect for authority is the price that each and every one of us must pay to achieve any goal that is worthwhile."[2]

## THE REIGNING PROCESS

Reigning, on the other hand, has to do with the power to exercise authority or influence over something or someone. All eight of Nick Saban's assistants who are now head coaches acknowledge him as their mentor and much of the reason for their success. Rick Godwin in his book *Training for Reigning*[3] suggested that the training and reigning that we must master as men has more to do with our character and maturity rather than over any other being. While I do not necessarily subscribe to the notion of "reigning over entities," such as a dictator or social situation where one person makes all the decisions without input from anyone else, I do believe that our character is a vital part of the reigning process in that we do not say one thing and then our actions demonstrate something different.

Former Virginia Tech head football coach, Frank Beamer in his book *Let Me Be Frank*, states that, "Champions do not become champions when they win the event, but in the hours, weeks, months, and years they spend preparing for it. The victorious performance itself is merely the demonstration of their championship character."[4] In addition, I believe character is who we are when no one is watching us, but our reputation is who we are when others are around. The sad commentary is that many are more concerned with their reputation. This can be a sensitive subject and can evoke many emotions, but at some point, we must grow up and put away childish things if we are going to have dominion over the things that God has put in our charge (I Corinthians 13:11). The realm of influence for some may be larger than others, but the fact remains that we are all called to lead by example first. We cannot tell others to love and pray for those in leadership and then we join the haters who criticize and complain about what the leaders are or are not doing that we deem to be not in our best interests. Also, we cannot suggest the importance of sacrificing time to attend functions at school and other civic events when we never take the time to show up at any of these events.

For some, this has become a lost art. This is not to suggest that there is an absence of leaders that lead by example. However, I would emphatically say that we fail to lead by example when it comes to admitting that we messed up and that we may need help. Even though we may disagree, life happens to all of us and to our families as well. Unfortunately, some think that leaders are immune to pain, struggles, disappointment, and abandonment. To those who have been a part of leadership and understand the training before the reigning, they will be the first to tell you that the same problems that people encounter in general, leaders experience as well. The only difference in the two is how we choose to react when things happen beyond our control. We can treat it as if we are above the situation or we can tell the masses the story of what happened, how we responded, and what lessons were learned.

### OUR GREATEST INFLUENCE IS AT HOME

I have found that my greatest level of influence starts and ends at home, as a father, husband, and provider. This took me a while to discover, but I am glad I did. For the most part, I believe we do well providing for our families, but as husbands we struggle. I believe this is due in part to the lack of examples or models before us. Because of this, I will say we all need another man who we can be transparent with. The late Ed Coles in his book *Maximize Manhood*[5] suggests that every man needs two men in their lives. They need an Abraham who they can look up to and model and a Timothy who they can pour into.

Although my father was a good example as a provider, he could not model the example of being a good husband. What I have found over the years is that when we expose ourselves to those who we can trust, that's when we can get help. I have been married for over thirty-four years and some have asked how did we survive? My answer is quite simple: it's a daily walk. In other words, there will be trials and tests. I made mistakes, but I admitted when I was wrong and tried to do better the next time. Also, I made a conscious, intentional decision not to make excuses to justify my actions. If I did something, said something, or went somewhere out of my anger, I tried to be accountable for all my actions.

Communication was an issue for me because I would just shut down and not say anything when I was angry, but it only hurt in the long run because it would create distance between us. After talking with a counselor, I realized that shutting down was just making matters worse and frustrating both of us because my wife wanted to know what was wrong and I wanted to keep everything to myself. After several sessions of counseling, I tried to always keep the lines of communication open by sharing when I was upset even if it took a day or two. Another step in opening the lines of communication is that I always try to ask my wife how was her day before discussing anything else with her.

I believe one of the worst things to happen when you don't take the time to build the relationship is once you enter the empty nest phase and are not sure of what to do next. In addition to feeling loneliness when children leave home for the first time, the empty nest syndrome can expose where there are some holes in your relationship with your spouse. I am usually very intentional about asking my wife how my son and daughter are doing particularly if I had not talked to them in a while. This normally stimulates additional discussion because there is always something going on with my son that we both need to address. On the other hand, my daughter is somewhat like me and tends to hold things in so I have to ask my wife how she is doing. This is when we really get into a deeper conversation because she then would say I need to call my daughter more often to find out for myself. Although at times thediscussion may be more about our children, it still keeps the lines of communication open with us.

The final thing I would say about marriage is that there will always be those who subscribe to various methods of a successful marriage, but we must remember that what works for one may not work for the other. I do believe there are keys to a lasting marriage. Some of those keys are learning how to compromise, a willingness to listen, a willingness to forgive, and not throwing in the towel when one messes up. I also believe that listening to those whom we trust and seeking counseling before and during a crisis is always helpful.

One of the worst things we can do as men when we are going through our struggles is to isolate ourselves. This only causes us to shut down, creating other issues that make it difficult to communicate with our spouse. As a side note, there is nothing wrong with counseling if both parties agree. I believe one of the most aggravating things for a wife is to desire counseling but the husband refuses to share. No matter how much the wife shares, the session won't be as beneficial because the counselor will only see one perspective. Therefore, for the counseling to be productive both must agree to be open, honest, and transparent. In my case I initially refused, but later consented and the sessions were very fruitful.

While my marriage had its challenges, it was just as difficult finding out my daughter was pregnant right after she had completed her undergraduate studies. To make matters worse, I was the last to find out she was pregnant. As a pastor and leader in a very small community, I felt embarrassed, angry, and hurt. Initially, I did not know what to say to my daughter. However, after praying, the Lord spoke to me before I met with my daughter. My conversation with the Lord really was short and sweet. It was not long and drawn out as some may think with him reminding me of times in my life when he spared me. He simply said, "Blessed are the merciful for they shall obtain mercy; now you take it from there." He also cautioned me that how I handled this situation would chart a new course for my life and the ministry. It would help me to be able to minister to other unwed young mothers having experienced the situation first hand. It would also teach me as a leader to be more sympathetic with others when they make mistakes. Finally, as a father, this situation taught me that supporting my daughter at one of the most crucial times in her life far outweighed any embarrassment I may have felt because of my position in the community. I realized that I am a father first and as such we cannot allow what we do to dictate who we are.

When my daughter finally told me she was pregnant, she was crying as she tried to explain it to me. I stopped her in the middle of crying and told her this: "Baby girl, pastoring is what I do, but a father is who I am. As long as God allows me to live, I will be your father first, period." I assured her that we all make mistakes and that you do not have to live your whole life trying to make up for what you did wrong. I assured her that I would deal with the church and that was not her battle to fight. Not so much for what she did or what the church may think, but that my daughter needed the support of her father not her pastor. Since she had just graduated from college, I encouraged her to still pursue her career while letting her know we would be there throughout the pregnancy. Whatever she needed during the pregnancy, I tried to be there. From doctor's visits to just checking in on her each day. Needless to say, from that time until now, I believe that was perhaps the most significant thing I did as a father with my daughter, and that makes me proud. Furthermore, because of the support I gave to my daughter, I am a proud grandfather who looks forward to my grandson spending the entire summer with his Papa.

### DEFINING MOMENTS

There will always be defining moments in our lives, and it's not always just what we say that matters in the end; it's what we say *and* do that ultimately speaks to the masses we lead. As a pastor and community leader to so many, it was my actions with my daughter that I believe garnered more respect in the eyes of my parishioners rather than me trying to defend or justify her pregnancy. Menspiration has more to do with us sharing our experiences openly and honestly in a forum where others get a chance to see you for who you are not just for what we do. When we do this, others will become transparent as well and began to share their stories and in the process of time we all began to reign over our unique kingdoms with integrity and truth.

For some reason, many of us have lost the art of embracing the jewels that are birthed from the truth. Those jewels are sometimes those who were born out of wedlock or out of what some call a "mistake" who later become great leaders, trail blazers, and game changers. What some may have thought was trash become those treasures in earthen vessels that the apostle Paul referred to in his writing (2 Corinthians 4:7). Jesus asserts that truth is a liberator (John 8:32). He further adds that when you know the truth it makes us free: free from the bondage of what others may think, free from the bondage of our past, free from the bondage of our failures, and finally, free from our own attempt to commit spiritual suicide. We commit spiritual suicide when we deliberately attempt to sabotage our own destiny because we become bound by what others say or feel about us. As a result, we allow others to define us.

### REALITY CHECK

So, we must remember that some of the same people that were compassionate to us when we were in our storm want the same justice and mercy when they are in their storm. It is amazing how things shift when the shoe is on the other foot. However, the test of our character is not only how we treat them, but also how we respond to the criticism of others who did not like how those same individuals treated us. My response to these individuals was plain and simple: "Blessed are the merciful for they will obtain mercy."

Although sometimes we want to lash out at those who did not show us mercy, we must remember that it is always bigger than us. We are not responsible for what people do to us but what we do to them. It was a great opportunity for me to witness to these individuals, not so much in word, but in deeds and actions. Though these kinds of situations may not happen every day, if we can remember it's just training for what we may encounter in the future, we will grow as leaders. After all, we are the authors of our destiny, and we must not let others write or change our story.

**TRUTH MOMENT**
I recall as a sophomore in high school going to my guidance counselor to inquire about college. She asked had any of my siblings or parents attended college. I told her no, and she said I should not spend a lot of time worrying about going to college. This was a defining moment for me because I almost allowed what my guidance counselor thought about my family's experience to dictate where I was going in my future. She believed she was really helping me by suggesting that I shouldn't worry about attending college, but in actuality she was trying to hijack my story. So many of us have had others—even those in trusted positions—tell us what they thought was best for us, only to end up short changing our dreams and destiny. Although I was the first in a family of six to go to college, it almost did not happen because of someone who judged my future based on my family history. She had good intentions, but good intentions have never won any awards. Only those who started and finished win those most coveted awards such as magna cum laude or summa cum laude.

CHAPTER 3

# Our Narrative as Men
Writing Your Own Story

Like most young men growing up in the city, my dream was to become the next Sam Jones, Casey Jones, or even Bill Russell. I know I'm probably dating myself, but these guys were basketball stars back in the late sixties and seventies who played for the Boston Celtics®. I know some of you are saying why not Michael Jordan; well I will get to him in a later chapter. At any rate, that was my dream and aspiration, and for a while I thought it could possibly come true. However, as time would progress, and I grew no taller than 5 feet 7 inches, I began to focus my energies on other professions. The point I'm trying to make was that I wrote my own story.

While I am a dreamer, I am also a realist, and the odds of me making it to the NBA as a five-foot-seven-inch point guard was slim at best. While I know there were a few who did make it—Calvin Murphy, Spud Webb, and Muggsy

Bogues—they were the exception and not the rule. I realized that I needed a back-up plan if I did not make it to the league.

While it's important to dream big and shoot for the stars, we must also have a back-up plan so that we don't get stuck in a time warp, where our past or future becomes our present. When this happens, we get caught up in the name game, blame game, or shame game. With the name game, we begin to mention certain names to others hoping they will think that because we know or knew someone, it explains why we are where we are today. On the other hand, with the blame game, we start to blame our current state on others as if this will excuse why things have not changed in our lives. Finally, we play the shame game hoping that our friends will have pity on us because of certain bad breaks we might have experienced which led to our present state of being. These things may very well be true, but at the end of the day, we are still responsible and accountable to write our own story.

### Whose Report Do We Believe

When I think back to that morning of my sophomore year in high school when my guidance counselor told me I was not college material, I had two choices: I could either believe what she said or write my own story. Now as a sixteen year old, writing my own story was a tall order, especially when I only had one goal in mind of going to the NBA. However, thank God my guidance counselor was not the only person I sought for guidance.

We should never be afraid to seek out others for help; we all need a support group. This is not to suggest that we are addicted to anything, but it is great to have that go-to person you can contact and receive a second opinion. Also, it is a good thing to have other men in your life to give you a different perspective on things we may have only seen one way. Second opinions are always recommended when you are about to make critical decisions in your life. It is not that you do not trust your go-to person but there is safety in the multitude of counsel.

## WE ALL NEED A COACH

Although my coach was well versed in basketball, I soon found out that he was just as good about life. When I approached him to get his thoughts about me going to college, it was amazing how he seemed to know what I needed to hear. He didn't just tell me what I wanted to hear, but he shared his story and how he had similar struggles. I believe what we all need to hear when we are unsure about something is that somebody else has faced similar struggles, but they made it through. Somehow hearing another person's story may confirm what we are thinking, but it also gives us the confidence to fight or move forward.

My coach not only shared his story, but reassured me that I could and would be successful in college. This was monumental to me, because outside of my father, my coach was the only other man that I really looked up to and respected. Not to mention I played basketball under him for four years in high school. He not only coached me but spent time with me over the summer to make sure I stayed out of trouble. This was critical for me because during the summer of my freshman year, I experienced a tragedy with my oldest brother, and I thought I would never be able to play basketball again in high school. But it was what my coach did off the court that really saved my life.

We must remember that for some kids the only person they will ever see as a father is the coach. So, whether we like it or not, as coaches, our influence extends far beyond the nets and basketball, but into the home, the classroom, the playground, and ultimately the courts of life. I am just grateful that my coach took the time to invest in me outside of his normal basketball duties and helped me to understand the x's and o's of life, and how to be a point guard at home. Being a point guard at home meant taking the lead when critical decisions had to be made and not expecting others to do for me what I could do for myself. This would be pivotal in me changing the game and winning in life not just on the court. As a side note, not only did my coach encourage me to attend college, but he helped me move in on the first day of school.

### How Do We Give Back?

With all that my coach did for me to be the first person in my family to attend and finish college, I really wanted to find a way to give back to others. I believe we all have a moral and civic responsibility to give back when we have been blessed by others. The notion that we stand on broad shoulders is no good if we, who are beneficiaries, do not pay it forward. As much as I would like to give back to one of my greatest mentors, Coach George B. Lancaster, I am sure he would simply say, "Do for somebody else as it was done for you."

Menspiration is all about giving back and telling your story in hopes of helping others in the process of their stories being written. If sharing my story regarding what I experienced during a critical time in my marriage or while raising my children will help one to navigate through their process, then mission accomplished. Even though our stories or experiences may be different, we still can glean some truth for where we may be going. A closer look at the process would show us that we all have something to share; it's just that we need some others on the team to help us navigate through the process. Maybe if my guidance counselor never told me that I was not college material, I would have never sought the advice of my coach. Maybe if I never sought the advice of my coach, I would have never become a coach in a town I said I would never return.

In a perfect world, we all would love to say we did it our own way on our own terms and that we never needed help to accomplish what we have today. Well, we all know that we do not live in a perfect world, but we do serve a perfect God who is perfect in all of his ways. Therefore, he allows all of us a measure of success not to keep it to ourselves, but if by chance we cross the path of others who need assistance along the way, we would oblige them. The challenge, however, is if we are willing to give back even to those who we may feel do not deserve what we have to offer. Moreover, are we willing to look beyond a person's faults and see their need? If the answer is yes to both of those questions than I believe the game is changing for all of us and *Menspiration* is speaking to all of us.

My struggle in writing this book is that there are other books in the marketplace with a similar subject matter, so why would there be a need for another one. Well what changed my mind was the fact that so many have made similar statements, such as, "My vote will not make a difference . . . I'm just one person." We know the consequences of those kind of statements; we are suffering now as a nation. One vote matters; your story matters. Write it; someone will read it!

**Truth Moment**

As I look back over my life, the one thing I regret is that I did not tell my story earlier. We look for affirmation and validation from certain people, only to realize that what we have to say is just as important. The truth is that our context in sharing our story will resonate with people who have had similar issues, but what helps them with what they are going through is knowing they are not alone in the process. What helped me through the fear of perhaps failing and not finishing college was knowing that others battled some of the same issues. In addition, the willingness of others to share their story became a model for me not just during the times of my struggles, but later on in life. Sometimes we fail to realize that life is a combination of seasons and cycles, wins and losses,

# MENSPIRATION

ups and downs, summers and winters. The key, however, is knowing the seasons and cycles we may be in life. One final thought: coaching does not end with your current season, it carries over to the offseason. After hanging up my sneakers over forty years ago, I still call my coach today for advice. In fact, he was instrumental in me making the decision to undergo knee surgery.

## Chapter 4

# Shifting the Paradigm
*Willing to Do the Difficult Things*

Someone defined insanity as repeating the same mistakes over and over again but expecting different results. As bizarre as this may sound, there are those who still have not received the memo and don't understand why life has not changed for them. It is important that we see that shifting the paradigm does not mean we are out of the loop all together, but rather it is about a collective and collaborative approach to get more men on board to share their stories to help all of us become better fathers, husbands, and mentors. Over the last twenty years, I have watched the phone industry along with technology change the game of communication to the point where I almost feel lost without my cell phone. It was not until recently I made an intentional decision to go off the grid with my phone on Saturdays in hopes of spending some time with me! Choosing to turn off my cell phone one weekend out of every month has helped me detoxify from my cell phone addiction! It was a difficult decision, but I had to garner enough discipline to simply do it. As time passed, I realized that I could not only live without my cell phone, but I actually enjoyed the me time. Of all the things that have changed over the years, the one thing that has captured my attention is that we all have become consumed with devices, such that we have lost the art of spending time with the ones behind the devices.

Sure, the paradigm has shifted from home phones to cell phones, but the challenge for many of us is not to allow them to consume us. Some things take time to adjust to, especially when you are used to doing things a certain way for so long. For example, my best chance in communicating with my son today is to text him first in hopes of him at least reading it on the go and then responding appropriately. Unfortunately, it does not always work because many times he is driving, and I hate for him to text while he is driving. I will say that for the most part I do receive a quicker response from him when I text rather than call him. As the older generation still prefers to talk and the younger generation prefers to text, you must be willing to make some adjustments to how you function if you want to be a player in the game. However, the relevant question for some of is how do you make the change when you are playing with outdated equipment?

### Update Your Equipment

Over the course of my life I have had the privilege of working with some great leaders. One of the finest in Brunswick, VA is Bryant Stith. As one of his assistant coaches, I witnessed an exceptional coach, scholar, and great person. What really blessed me was his willingness to make sure the team was always on the cutting edge of the latest basketball equipment and gear. I never forget one day coming into the gym seeing this tall piece of equipment that look like a statue. I later found out that it was a shooting machine. Remember, I played high school basketball back in the mid-seventies, and the only shooting machine I ever witnessed was a fellow on our team who almost broke his wrist from shooting so much! In fact, he never saw a shot in a game that he did not like or that he thought he could not make.

At any rate, Coach Stith invested his own money into buying the team a shooting machine and it made all the difference in the world. We went to eight consecutive state championships, winning the last three, before Coach Stith moved to the college ranks. Now I am sure some of you may have asked did the shooting machine really make that much of a difference, and my answer is no doubt. It not only gave the players a chance to use some of the latest equipment to better their game—some even stayed hours after practice to shoot around—but it also showed the players that coach was willing to invest in them as individuals.

I'm sure some teams have won plenty of games using outdated equipment and not having the latest shooting machine, but sometimes it's about working smarter not harder. When you have a coach that recognizes your potential and has the willingness to invest his time, talent, and finances into you as a person and as a team, it really makes all the difference. Now on a larger scale, we must be willing to invest in our future by updating our financial planning to include insurance policies, personal development, and overall health awareness. For example, over the last few years, I have buried too many young men with no insurance policy or personal will leaving their spouses and family with funeral and other expenses too large for them to handle. As hard as many of us work, it is no reason why we cannot update our financial portfolio by putting a few dollars aside on a term or whole life insurance policy which would at least protect your family from future financial hardship. We have to stop placing the burden of our future on our loved ones and become more financially responsible.

### It's Worth the Investment

Sometimes we all ask the question is it worth the investment, particularly when we do not see immediate returns. However, none of us would be where we are today if someone had not taken the time to make a deposit in our lives. Menspiration is a result of that deposit made in my life: men that are motivated in spite of their individual struggles, but also inspired by other men who were transparent while going through similar struggles. Together we mend and blend our efforts to be the men that were made in the image of our Father. At the end of the day, we all are stronger and hopefully wiser because we did not carry the load by ourselves. The time we spend with one person might be the one-time investment that prevents suicide, giving up in school, quitting a relationship, or just saying I cannot do this anymore.

    I am reminded of a time I invested in a young man's life while he was still incarcerated. I visited him one Saturday afternoon, not knowing that he would be released a month later. Upon his release, he contacted me while I was dealing with a tragedy in my family. Although I tried to rush him off, he insisted in wanting to share his testimony with me. I finally agreed, and he told me that the day I visited him he was planning on committing suicide, but my words changed his life forever. Today he is a leader and motivational speaker, and to think I had that kind of impact just by investing a few hours on a Saturday afternoon to share some words of encouragement with a young man, is simply amazing. Too often we allow yesterday's problems to rob us of today's opportunities, and tomorrow to hijack our possibilities for the present. Let's maximize the moments, because we never know the impact it may have on someone's tomorrow.

### Lost Opportunities

We can unwittingly become the wounded healer just by taking advantage of the opportunities that present itself to us at the time. By listening to the young man's testimony, it became the remedy for my pain. I had gotten caught up in my pain such that I did not realize that part of my healing was just in listening to his testimony. If we were to take the time to scan our memory banks we would be surprised to discover the number of opportunities we lost by not doing something intentional such as stopping to say a kind word to someone.

> *Too often we allow yesterday's problems to rob us of today's opportunities, and tomorrow to hijack our possibilities for the present.*

What I'm finding out with each day that is in front of me is that the window of opportunity gets shorter and shorter simply because the years I have in front of me are so much shorter than those behind me. This by no means is a suggestion that my best days are behind me, but rather a reality check that the more times I miss doing something that is intentional or perhaps life changing for someone else, I minimize the possibility of that day being one of the best days of my life. We all want it to be said one day long after we are gone that we made a difference in somebody's life, no matter how great or small. This perhaps is why we cannot go another day saying I could have, would have, or should have done something about a particular situation.

You may recall the story about the man who was on the seashore just tossing starfish after starfish back into the sea. After about an hour, a younger gentleman who had been running along the shore, came up to the older gentleman and said, "Sir, you know it's over a thousand starfish on the shore, and you'll be here all day trying to make a difference." The older gentleman politely turned around after tossing another one back into the sea and said to the younger fellow, "Well, I made a difference in this one's life." The moral of the story is that to make a difference in the world, we must do it one person at a time. We will always have those who we meet every day trying to stop us. Do not allow others to discourage you; start today and make the difference.

**TRUTH MOMENT**
Sometimes doing the most difficult things when the paradigm is shifting is not popular. Taking over as head coach after eight years of being a successful assistant, was one of the toughest decisions of my life. I told Coach Stith that he set me up because myself and the other coaches decided that when he stepped down we would all leave at the same time. I later found out that Coach Stith told the principal that I was the only one he thought could keep the basketball program at Brunswick High School moving forward. After hearing that statement, I started sweating bullets because of the pressure it put on me. But I accepted the challenge and coached for another three years.

Another one of the toughest decisions I had to make was letting go one of our star players because he would not conform to the culture of what I was trying to develop in these young men. It was not just about basketball, but about character, integrity, and academic excellence. The day is over where we cover for the superstar athlete who has failing grades, questionable character, and is a constant behavioral problem. I knew I would get some push back from my coaches and even from some parents because I set the bar high. So, when I finally told the young man there was no need for him to come out for basketball, he was disappointed. Although I explained to him my decision, he still wanted to play. I told him it was a tough decision but it was final. To make a long story short, we still won the district and regional championship, but we loss in the state tournament. Things may have turned out differently with the young man still on the team, but I had no regrets. In the end, winning for me was secondary and character development was primary. Somebody must be willing to do the difficult things when the paradigm is shifting.

## Chapter 5

# Pursuing your Passion
*So What You Messed Up*

Passion has been defined as more than just enthusiasm and excitement, but ambition that is materialized into action. I have always believed that there are three types of people in the world: the pessimist, those that watch things happen; the opportunist, those that make things happen; and the realist, those that don't know what happened. While it takes all three to make up the world, only those that are passionate about their pursuit in life generally make things happen.

James, the brother of Jesus, was a little blunter about people; he said there are really two types of people, hearers and doers (James 1:22). Hearers tend to procrastinate, while doers celebrate because they get it done. Regardless of the group we may fall in, I think we would all agree that if you do not have the ambition to do something, more than likely you won't do anything.

I have always been asked how I get so many things done each day. My response is there are twenty-four hours in a day and you must maximize each moment while pursuing your passion. Maximizing your moments means you do not allow distractions or small things to stop you from your overall purpose. Furthermore, even when you mess up along the way, you keep it moving so you do not lose focus. At one point in my life, I was finishing up my dissertation toward a doctorate in education, head basketball coach and dean of students at my high school, and the senior pastor of a growing church in Virginia. While I could have stopped because it was hard at times, I still continued to pursue my passion. I would not listen to the pessimists who said I was crazy or the realists who questioned my purpose. However, when it was all said and done, I accomplished everything I set out to do. Of course, I had some setbacks along the way, but they did not prevent me from coming back to finish what I started my sophomore year in high school. Sometimes when we are told what we cannot do it becomes the fuel to conquer the world. Although I might not have conquered the world, walking across that stage receiving my doctorate degree and hood, sure felt like I did.

To help me maximize each moment and maintain balance with every responsibility and obligation I had, I kept a weekly checklist and stayed true to it. If I had a paper due during the same week I had a game, I made sure I completed the paper a week before the deadline. I never waited to the last minute to complete assignments or prepare for sermons. Preparation was my secret weapon! I always planned ahead of time by reviewing the basketball schedule, my course syllabus, and pastoral engagements. Many times it was tight, and I had to burn the midnight oil occasionally, I got it done because I wanted to get it done. As a husband and father, my wife was very understanding and worked with me because she knew I had a goal in mind. On weekends we set aside a day for each other and made up for any lost time. By and large it was a great feat, but planning, avoiding distractions, and having a great support group really made the difference. Even when you get off schedule on some days, do not allow it to stop you from pushing forward.

### So What if You are a Late Bloomer

What is so amazing about my story is that some would say I was a late bloomer; I accomplished all of this on the other side of fifty. Now when I turned fifty, I did not say I would be a head coach or that I would start to work on my doctorate degree. Sometimes when opportunity and destiny meet, we have to be bold enough to at least say, as Mordecai said to Esther, "Who knows whether or not you have come to the kingdom for such a time as this" (Ester 4:14). We never know when and where God is positioning us for our next assignment, so it is always best to be prepared.

When I look back over coaching and working on my dissertation, they both helped me in becoming a better pastor. Although the work was strenuous at times, the process of recognizing problems, developing a literary review, determining a methodology, gathering results, and discussing recommendations, proved to be invaluable at the end of the day. The time spent on research and scholarly articles helped in my development of sermon writing. I became more detailed in my messages. In determining what methodology to use, qualitative or quantitative research, I eventually went with a quantitative approach because it involved random sampling. In doing so it helped me to witness to people at random and to share the gospel on occasions. In order to get a reasonable sampling pool, you had to ask a lot of people. As a result, I asked a lot of people about the subject matter I was dealing with, and I also invited them to church. Sometimes we are reluctant to witness and invite people to Christ, but working on my quantitative research helped me during this process.

Late bloomers may not always be the first out of the gate, but when they do come out, you know that they are in the game.

During the second year of my coaching tenure, I was approached by another coach who complimented me on the way that my guys carried themselves on and off the court. I responded to the coach in a gracious manner but assured him that it did not happen overnight; it was a process. Furthermore, I told him that it was a culture change and that when the guys buy in to the culture, they become better players, better students, and better young men. If we are ever going to change the mindset of those around us, we must be willing to address the culture or the behavior of those we encounter. We must not forget that we are products of our environment. It is a true statement that what we allow we promote. If we allow young men to be disrespectful, arrogant, and not appreciative of the opportunity to compete, then we are promoting a very toxic culture that eventually will become the norm and not the exception. Even as a late bloomer, I learned that success is still accomplished if we work hard, be persistent, and never give up when it looks like things are the worst.

### So, What's Really Driving You?

If most people knew what drives us, they would really be surprised. I asked a close friend who is rather wealthy, what was the one thing that drives him every day, and he said the fear of failure. This really shocked me because on the outside he appeared to be successful and without any cares in the world. However, for some of us, fear has been the underlying force that keeps us from moving forward. So what you messed up! We read too many stories about multi-millionaires, famous athletes, or successful businessmen who messed up and failed, but didn't allow their failures to stop them.

I remember working with my dad as a waiter at John Marshall Hotel during the early seventies. At that time most of the major political events were hosted at the hotel. Usually, about twenty to thirty waiters would work on any given

## So What You Messed Up

night to serve during the events. One night I was responsible for serving thirty individuals who sat at four tables. Although I was a little scared having to carry twelve dinner plates stacked three high, I managed to get through dinner. However, for dessert we had the famous *flaming cherries jubilee*; it was the talk of the night. Imagine cherries simmered with brown sugar, topped with brandy, and a scoop of vanilla ice cream. When I came out of the kitchen I was already a little scared, and when I arrived at the table, I dropped my tray spilling all the ice cream on a customer, who was obviously disgusted by the situation. I knew my dad would holler at me for spilling the ice cream on one the biggest nights at the hotel. It was no secret that my dad would respond this way because he was always tough on us growing up. He expected the best from us always with no exceptions, and I was afraid.

I can recall growing up when he would come home from work and all of us would scatter like roaches because we knew he would find something wrong when he would come into the house. Of course, if the house was not clean or we had got into any trouble, he would holler at us. Because of this, I try to be conscious of my hollering, but I'm not always successful. On one occasion I was hollering at my son on the phone because of something he had done, and he hung up. My response to him when I called him back was not pleasant." At any rate, with this in the back of my mind, it's no wonder why I spilled ice cream on a customer.

We never know the kind of negative impact we have on our sons when we don't give them the space to make mistakes. Moreover, much of how we treat our sons today is based on our context of how we were raised. I now see why I was so critical of my son, as the apple doesn't fall too far from the tree. However, on the night that I spilled the ice cream, it turned out to be a defining moment for me with my father. Not only did my father cover for me, but he told me afterwards he was proud of me for coming back out to serve the other guests even after I failed the first time. We all have failed or messed up at one time or another in life; however, the key is knowing how to turn failure into success. After looking back over my life and particularly this story of me making this huge mistake, I recognized the one thing that was driving me was the search for my dad's approval. I tried so hard that night not to make a mistake so that he would be proud of me, but I messed up anyway. The beauty, however, was that because I did not give up when I messed up, I still got the approval of my dad. My drive for affirmation from my father almost cost me my job that night. Maybe my son's drive not to disappoint me on the basketball court led him to start drinking. At any rate, all of us are driven by something.

## There are No Free Passes to Success

For some strange reason there are those who think reading a book, going to a seminar, a workshop, or even following a ten-step approach will make one successful. While all of these are tools to success, work must be applied; in fact, it takes hard work to be successful in life. No building or great structure was erected with tools alone; someone had to use those tools and apply their skills to complete the structure. It is the same concept with taking pills or any other formula to lose weight or live a healthy life; they are only supplemental to our success. If we don't walk and exercise, the pills and formula cannot do it alone. At some point, hard work and discipline has to be a part of the equation if we want to maintain a healthy lifestyle.

Watching some of the exercise videos and seeing the results may fool you into thinking it happened overnight. However, upon close examination—especially if you tried it—you soon find out that the pounds just don't fall off, they have to be *worked* off. Moreover, it's not a one-time situation, but an ongoing process. Even after I watched the Insanity® workout video, I concluded that one must be insane if they believe they can work out like that for a short time and stay in shape. The truth is that there is no easy pass or free pass to success. To maintain your weight or stay on top of your game, there is no way around hard work and just getting it done. NBA player Kevin Durant stated it best: "Hard work beats talent." I might also add that hard work helps us maintain our successful lifestyle even when our gifts and talent fade with time.

### Truth Moment

During the last semester of my doctoral coursework, I was working on my dissertation at the same time. I submitted my final dissertation review to my departmental chair and he denied me three times. In fact, I called him and almost cursed him out along with wanting to quit the program. Yes, the good old reverend /pastor/community leader of twenty-five years, wanted to curse my chair out. I felt that the minor changes he wanted me to make were changes he could have made. He even had the nerve to say, "You are almost there, just hang in there." I made the changes and I still did not meet the final approval. Anyone who has ever worked on a dissertation knows that the process is never over until the chair says it's over.

> *Hard work helps us maintain our successful lifestyle even when our gifts and talent fade with time.*

After about four or five more edits, I finally received approval. I could have easily given up and forgotten it and said at least I finished my coursework. However, in the back of my mind, I thought about my high school counselor once again, who probably would have said, *Do not worry about it Ronald, nobody in your family completed their doctorate either.* Now you can imagine how I was really feeling, like I was in between a rock and a hard place. I also considered the statistics that showed the number of African Americans who finish their coursework, but never complete their dissertations. (They are known as "ABDs . . . All But Dissertation.") I did not want to be included in that number. So, I buckled down, did a gut check, and the rest was history. In 2014, I received my doctorate degree in Educational Leadership from Nova Southeastern University. There was no easy pass, no free pass, and no senior citizen pass; I earned it, by the grace of God.

CHAPTER 6

# Inspiration versus Frustration
*A New Perspective on Getting it Done*

One of the most frustrating things I encountered while growing up is never being able to please my father. During my junior and senior year of high school, I worked with my father as a waiter at a hotel where he basically did everything including the hiring and firing. Since I was still in high school, there were days I asked to be off because of a game or something else that had to do with school. Of course, he did not really chew me out, but I knew he was not pleased because he always wanted me to be there to learn what to do in the event he had to leave me in charge.

Towards the end of my senior year in high school, my father finally would leave me in charge of the night crew after his day shift. On one particular occasion, I calculated the wrong gratuity for a party, and the next day my father let me have it. I could handle being wrong, but it was as if I could do nothing right. He finally sat down with me one day and showed me how to calculate the tax, gratuity, and hotel fee. It seemed simple after he walked me through it, but I guess he thought since I was a junior in high school I should have known the difference between 15, 4, or 2 percent of a hotel bill. I guess that's why today I have no problem after dining out giving the waiter 20 or 22 percent for gratuity. As frustrating as this was working for and with my dad, it somehow inspired me later when I got to college. Not only did I learn work ethics from my father, but he did not give me a break just because I was his son. Actually, I believe he was preparing me for the work force and at the same time showing me that I could always get a job as a banquet waiter. It was hard work, but it was also rewarding if you did a good job serving people.

**THERE IS NOTHING WRONG WITH SERVING BUT . . .**
I think it's great to serve other men. However, like anything, it can be taken too far at times. I believe armor-bearers and adjutants are needed in the church, but I also believe they should not only serve the leadership but the laity as well. In biblical days, armor-bearers and adjutants were individuals who carried the shield and large weapons of a king (1 Samuel 14:7). It was usually one individual who attended to the king concerning these matters. However, today there are about three or more who carry everything from the Bible to the socks of leaders. One or two is fine, but five or ten or an entourage is a bit too much. Because of the large number of armor-bearers accompanying some leaders, much of the attention is diverted from the leader and the focus becomes the entourage, when their original aim is to serve in the background. I do not say this with any ill will but simply to point out that genuine service is not limited to rank, but to whoever and wherever there is a need within the church.

I can recall going to a worship service and several brothers wanted to take my bag and my iPad®, and I politely told them it's not that heavy and that I can handle it. I was not trying to be rude, but I wanted them to know that it was not the things on the outside that I need help with, but some of those spirits on the inside such as hate, envy, and strife that nobody could see. By praying for me regarding those evil spirits, they would be helping me far more than just carrying my Bible or iPad®. Now that is getting the job done and taking the role of the armor-bearer to another level. This level involves praying for the minister and the parishioners that the word of God would fall on good ground or receptive hearts.

Growing up in the church, I saw so many brothers trying to get next to the pastor by carrying his bag and Bible, and I thought to myself, *Surely his bag and Bible cannot be that heavy.* When I got older, I asked the pastor to explain to me the role of an armor-bearer. Of course, it has evolved over the years, with some preferring to use the term *adjutant*. The essence of what I would like to convey is if we are going to serve, let it be in an inconspicuous manner simply because you love the idea of serving.

## LOOKS CAN BE DECEIVING

Sometimes we are inspired to do things because of what it looks like from the outside, but when we get closer, we find out that it is a different cup of tea. I have always desired to be a head coach, especially after my playing days were over and I realized that I was not going to the NBA. It intrigued me for several reasons: I felt that I could impact young men spiritually and athletically, I always liked the idea of walking the sidelines during a game and telling the referee they made a bad call, and I respected and admired my coach.

I got the opportunity when Coach Stith was offered another job at the college level. When I was offered the job, I really was not interested, but after some gentle convincing I accepted. Although my tenure as head coach lasted for only three years, it was perhaps the most fun I had in a long time. From the outside, I'm sure many thought I was a great coach to be able to step in after Bryant, who had been to eight consecutive state finals and won the last three. But looks can really be deceiving. Actually, it was my assistant coaches who did most of the work; I was just the eyes steering the ship.

Most times we tend to think it is the person out front doing the work, but usually it's those behind the scenes who are the nuts and bolts of the operation. It's just like the house that looks amazing after being built. We see the siding, the shutters, and the windows, and everything looks great. However, it is the foundation that nobody sees that is supporting the house. Although I was the visionary and gave the command, it was my supporting cast that got the job done. The frustration for some was that they hear those out front getting all the accolades but because they were always in the trenches they never received the same level of notoriety.

In addition, at times it was frustrating to call a play in the huddle after much work practicing that play, only to have the young men do what they wanted to do because the play was not flashy enough or wouldn't have the fans singing their praise. Of course, if we score, it's great, but if it results in a turnover, you are upset at the one that messed up. However, my inspiration and frustration came at the same time when I got the opportunity to play against my mentor and former coach, George Lancaster. I was so inspired just to be on the same sideline with him, but soon I became frustrated because we had come back from a fifteen-point deficit only to still lose the game.

The beauty was that even though we lost, being able to compete on the same stage and at the same level was a testament to what my coach put in me. Menspiration has much to do with how well we transfer to others what we have learned and what was instilled in us. Furthermore, when we are transparent with those who we mentor, it's not a crime to see them exhibit skills similar to ours. Being able to stand toe to toe with my former coach was not to say I had arrived but to say he taught me well. What I learned from him could never be measured by wins or losses. The fact that my players could see the man who mentored and coached me gave them a closer look at me. His team was disciplined, well coached, and exhibited great sportsmanship. Much of who I am has to do with discipline, being well coached, and always displaying the highest level of sportsmanship.

### CLOTHES DO MAKE A DIFFERENCE

As a first-year coach of a basketball team with a rich tradition for winning, I implemented a new dress code as a part of our program that season. My challenge was not only to continue the winning tradition, but to prepare those young men for life after basketball, and more importantly, success in the classroom.

To meet the challenges, my first assignment was to change the look or some of the ways of the program. Much of the behavior of many of the young men that year had been shaped by the negative behavior throughout the school. Suspensions for discipline issues were high during my first year as coach. Therefore, in hopes of changing this behavior, I implemented a dress code on game days. Initially, it was frustrating because for the most part none of the players wanted to dress up. They felt like I was trying to get them to go to church. I even had one of the teachers to kid me and my coaching staff by calling us "Rev. and his deacons" because we were all dressed alike with the same blazers and neckties. As frustrating as this was for me as the new coach, I still believe that clothes do make a man. First impressions are lasting impressions. That initial frustration turned into excitement when four businesses agreed to sponsor the basketball team by helping to purchase blue sport coats, blue neckties, a white shirt, and grey pants. It was the responsibility of each team member to purchase black socks and black shoes. The sponsors commended the team after attending the first game with their outfits, and it encouraged me to keep up the good work.

All team members were required to wear this outfit on all away games and for our annual district tournament. On home games they could wear their sweat suits. Amazingly, I noticed that when they wore their blazers and ties to school on away game days, they did well academically, had no discipline problems, and they were complimented by everybody from the principal to their peers. In addition, on those away games, we won the game and they were complimented by other schools. Toward the end of the season, the entire team asked if they could wear their blazers and ties to all games, not just away games. Now this was the same group of guys who at the beginning of the season did not want to dress up at all.

While I know in all cases clothes do not make the man, I do believe that uniforms make a difference. When everyone is dressed the same, there are fewer distractions. Furthermore, in the case with school uniforms, the economic benefits for parents who struggle to keep up with the latest fashion for their children far outweigh any negative feedback from parents who choose not to participate in the dress code policy. Not to mention the safety aspect, such as when students may be bullied or teased because they may not have the latest fashions, as well as the social aspect, where the students feel an increased sense of belonging. I know that if this can happen with a basketball team during the first year, certainly it can happen with an entire school.

In a larger context, when we set aside time and days where we are intentional about ourselves from looking good to even feeling good, it changes our perspective on life. With all that we encounter almost weekly from the media and other social outlets such as the notion that some of us are dead beat dads or absentee fathers, we all need that time where we dress up for a day simply to say we deserve it and we earned it.

### We Never Know How the Tables May Turn

As excited as I was to be on the sidelines with my former coach, he was just as excited to have one of his former players coaching against him. We never know how the tables will turn in life. Just when we think things may be going one way, they turn on us in a positive way. Of course, I consulted Coach Stith before I took the job, and his famous words to me were, "If not now, then when ... if not here then where ... and if not you, then whom?" These words still resonate with me today. I felt like it was a tall order to follow him after such a stellar high school coaching career. His knowledge and passion for the game was second to none. One of the final things Coach Stith said to me before leaving was that I had to take the job because the train does not stop. Amazingly, Coach Lancaster said almost the exact same thing.

As much fun as I had in coaching, we must also know when it is time to pass the baton. After my third year, I knew the game was steadily changing and I became more frustrated because the kids were becoming less willing to put quality time into practice and more willing to challenge the coaches' authority, so I decided to step down. Although it was hard, I knew it was time. One of the hardest things to do as leaders is knowing when to step up, step back, and ultimately step down. I had stepped up on many occasions to give direction and vision to the program. Now it was time for me to step down so the program could move in another direction. Several months after stepping down, I felt like a load had been lifted off of me. Sometimes we do not grasp that we are carrying more than we should until we let some things go. By giving up coaching, it inspired me to spend more time with my grandson and daughter.

I have seen too many leaders, who for a host of reasons, stay too long and never give another person the opportunity to step up. Some stay too long because they have nothing else to do and coaching is their life. The risk in staying too long is that we may encounter health issues and become stressed to the point we cannot recover. In addition, by staying too long those who would desire to step up to coach may decline because of the loss of interest. However, the joy in stepping down is that we can still coach, but in a different capacity. Menspiration is about coaching in a different capacity, life coaching per se. Sharing our experiences with those younger coaches in hopes of helping them to navigate through tough seasons in life.

Several days after I stepped down from coaching, I was asked by a news reporter what were my thoughts on coaching. I responded that coaching was about three things: making adjustments, timing, and knowing your players. The late Myles Munroe shares in his book *Passing It On*[6] a story about a great track star who was revered and admired by so many in his country. However, at the track star's funeral, Munroe notice that he was buried with a baton in his hand. The tragedy was that batons are made to be passed on, not buried. How many leaders today are being buried with their batons instead of passing them on? I know there were others who wanted me to coach for another three to five years, but it was time to pass the baton. Menspiration is about sharing our story and passing it on to another brother in hopes of him picking up the baton and running with it.

**TRUTH MOMENT**
Although I was the head coach for only three years, one of the most frustrating things I encountered happened during my second year as coach. It was during the second half of a game, in which we were leading by twenty-five or thirty points. One of the fans hollered at me, "How long are you go-

ing to leave the starters in the game?" Instead of ignoring the fan, I hollered back, "Until we get up by forty." Now I know that was not the right thing to say, but by that time, I had lost it. My frustration was that I had planned to take the starters out anyway during the next foul or dead ball. However, the fan did not give me that opportunity, and before I knew it, I responded in frustration. To add insult to injury, all of my assistant coaches turned to me laughing and asked, "Rev., are you okay?" I finally calmed down, took the starters out, and we eventually won the game by twenty points. I never forgot that moment, neither did my coaches let me forget it. It was a Kodak® moment that I wished had never happened, but it did, and I had to live with it.

Sometimes in life we have those moments where we say something or do something out of frustration, but we cannot allow that moment to define us. Moreover, we cannot allow isolated incidents to cloud our overall judgment when it comes to making critical decisions. I could have kept my starters in the game and ran the risk of them getting injured in spite of what the fan was hollering at me. Although the fan was simply expressing his opinion, which they all have a right to do, I should not have taken it personally. At the end of the day, sometimes we have to block out the noise of others and keep doing what we were called to do. We have to be careful not to listen to the noise of outsiders and run the risk of missing our destiny and abandoning our purpose.

CHAPTER 7

# The Recovery Process
*Maintaining Our Healing*

For most of us, when we think of recovery, we think of returning to health after an illness or injury; for others it may mean returning to a normal state after a period of difficulty. In both cases, the definition is well defined and understood. However, the one thing I believe that is overlooked is the term *process*. To some, the word process may simply mean one action that leads to another action, and then it's over. But to others, including myself, it involves a series of actions and steps taken over a period of time to receive a desired end. This I believe is invaluable.

I can recall three major events that happened over the course of my life that required not only an understanding of the term process, but also trusting the process. The first incident occurred when I was a happy-go-lucky four year old. There was an old metal faucet on the side of our house where the knob had become bald because of the rust and continuous usage of the knob. It looked like something from World War II because the metal ridges were completely bald. It was so hard to turn on that you would almost cut yourself. On this hot summer day, I jumped off the porch not paying attention to where I would land. I landed on that outside water faucet and split my leg wide open from top to bottom. I can remember it as if it was yesterday. There was blood everywhere, and all my friends were screaming. As a result, I had to be rushed to the hospital in a cab because my dad could not drive at the time. When I arrived at the hospital, they immediately rushed me into surgery because I had loss so much blood. When I woke up about an hour later, I had eighteen stitches and my leg was hurting so bad that it felt like someone had dropped a ton of bricks on me. Some fifty years later, I still have the scars on my leg where I received the eighteen stitches to close the gash in my leg.

    Recovery is a process. It is systematic and ongoing with a desired end in mind. In my case, I had an open scar that required healing from the inside and outside, therefore, the process took longer. Over the next few months, it was painful to get up in the mornings. The bandage on my leg had to be changed every two hours due to the blood seeping through. To ensure that my leg would not get infected, each day my mother would clean the injured area, change the bandage, and then make sure I would elevate my leg to keep the swelling down. This process continued for about a month or so. However, after about three months, the blood eventually stopped seeping through the bandage and the stitches were finally removed. As happy as I was at that time, the recovery process was still not complete. I had to go through physical therapy to learn how to walk again. Finally, after about six months, I regained the ability to walk. Being able to play little league football again was another sign that I had finally healed.

Life, at times, can deal to all of us similar blows such as the tragic loss of a loved one, a divorce, or even being displaced from our home and family. In the process of recovering, we may have to wait until the pain subsides, get support from family and friends, and finally take it one day at a time. For some, this process may take days but for others it may take months or even years. Pain, especially emotional pain, cannot always be regulated by taking medication or some other form of over the counter prescription. In many cases it has to run its course. In addition, it may require alternative measures such as taking a trip to remove yourself from the immediate situation or talking to those who have experienced similar losses. Menspiration has much to do with sharing our stories and experiences in hopes of helping others through these kinds of struggles in their life. It's not a question if these kinds of challenges will happen, but rather when these challenges happen do we have a manual that can help us navigate through the process.

## Scars Remind Us But Don't Define Us

Although I could no longer feel the pain from the injury, I could still remember the event because of the scars. Scars will always remind us, but they do not have to define us. Although some scars may be deeper than others, such as a father failing to express his love to his sons, daughters or wife, not realizing the future impact on his family, or a son becoming addicted to alcohol and refusing to acknowledge it, we must remember to trust the healing process. It may take years to acknowledge the pain, gather the support from family and friends, but in the end the joy is knowing that what we went through did not stop us from coming through. I could have been afraid to participate in sports and other events because of the scars. However, after listening to others share their stories and coaches who inspired me along the way, I realized that my scars did not have to cripple me.

The second event that took place in my life involved hernia surgery. Now men you can imagine the pain that I encountered before, during, and even after the surgery. Using the bathroom, intimacy with my wife, and playing sports was very painful. What caused me to finally have surgery was the day I bent over to pick up a piece of paper and could not stand back up due to the sharp pain in my abdominal area. I believe I developed the hernia because of over exertion and straining myself. At that time in my life, I was coaching baseball, basketball, teaching, serving as senior pastor, and playing pickup basketball on the weekends. I have always been an active person, but this time I overdid it, to say the least.

> *In the end the joy is knowing that what we went through did not stop us from coming through.*

Sometimes we ignore the symptoms of overexertion, but it's important to recognize them before they rupture other areas of our lives. In my case, it severely ruptured parts of my abdominal area. Before the surgery, I could barely walk due to abdominal pain and the hernia protruding out at times. I lived with the pain for almost six months before I decided to go to the doctor for advice. How many times have we dealt with pain that has been protruding and leaking out to the point where it becomes difficult for us to walk? Others notice it as well, but it is up to us to go to the source where we can get the help we need.

At any rate I went to the doctor and he told me that I had an inguinal hernia. This is a common type of hernia in which a loop of the intestine protrudes directly through a weak area of the abdominal wall in the groin. In other words, it's very painful if we don't take care of it. So, my decision was simple: either I continue to live with the pain or have the surgery. I chose to have the surgery and everything seemed to be okay until something happened during the recovery period. Like any surgery, there is a time where you are instructed to rest, not lift more than five pounds, and do not drive. Well I obeyed two of the three instructions but decided to drive after a day. As a result, I ruptured the stitches, started to bleed, and had to be taken back to the hospital for minor surgery. The doctor asked me what happened, and I told him I decided to drive because I felt better. He quickly reminded me that just because I felt better did not mean that I was well enough to drive. In fact, due to the movement of my legs and feet while driving, it simply irritated and ruptured the area where I received my stitches.

Many times in life, we experience major and minor emotional and physical surgical procedures and we tend to think we can just resume our normal activities, only to relapse because we were not ready to return to that place in life so quickly. It's similar to the instructions on a prescription bottle when we have to take antibiotics for infections in our body. The instructions clearly tell us to take the medication for seven days even if we feel better after two days. We must remember to trust and follow the process so that we maintain our healing.

After about two months I could finally drive again, and I was able to resume some of my normal activities. I had to decide whether to continue what I had been doing or let some things go. I decided to stop coaching baseball and playing pickup ball on the weekends. Although I missed both, my body felt much more relaxed after letting them go. It is imperative that we know when to step back from some things and give up other things. We have to continue to seek the face of God, solicit the support from loved ones, and remain positive in spite of the situation. It may be painful and uncomfortable for a while, but if we follow the instructions of the master surgeon and endure the process, everything will work out in our favor.

## Don't Prolong Your Recovery by Being Hardheaded

As I thought about my being hardheaded, I am reminded that sometimes in doing so we can rupture things in our lives and create unnecessary bleeding that may cause permanent damage. By not following the doctor's instructions, my recovery took longer than expected. However, from that point forward; I followed the instructions, eventually recovered, and was able to return to my normal activities. Although it may sound elementary, by following simple instructions for the moment, it can prevent major problems in the future. Thank God the bleeding stopped, because the doctor was considering going back into my incision to see if the hernia had ruptured again, and that would start the healing process all over again.

How many times have some of us been given simple instructions, only to disobey them and create massive bleeding in our homes and particularly in our relationships? I know it is easier said than done, but when you don't follow instructions it can almost feel like you are hemorrhaging and don't know it. I have not always made the best decisions in my life even after being told more than one time. The unfortunate thing is that when we make bad choices, it can be like bursting a blood vessel in our families; it affects everyone. The ruptured vessel can create problems with our spouse, our children, and everyone connected to us.

I remember when I decided to invest in a laundromat because it seemed like a good idea as it was the only one in the area where we lived at the time. Instead of reading the fine print, I decided to take the word of the person who asked me since I knew him. My wife always told me regardless of who I know, when it comes to business, to trust no one. As time passed, I noticed the business getting slower and slower. Shortly after entering the business venture, the one college in town that supplied many of the customers closed its doors.

As a result, I lost a considerable amount of money. This created a rift between my wife and I because even though she did not say it, I could hear her in the back of my mind saying "I told you so." I knew I had made a bad decision but did not need any constant reminders. This decision had a snowball effect: it affected our finances regarding doing things at home and with our children, and it also affected us emotionally because at times I would shut down and stop communicating with my wife if I felt she was reminding me of the investment.

When I look back, I only wish I could have compartmentalized the bleeding. However, when the bleeding finally stopped, the damage had already been done. My wife was hurt, my children were hurt, and everybody around me felt the pain of my bad decision. As we know, when we lose a sufficient amount of blood, the effects can be life threatening. The recovery process has been long and hard. However, when you trust the process you continue to forge ahead and share your story in hopes of others benefitting from the mistakes you've made.

The third event that took place in my life that required healing and recovery involved my arthroscopic knee surgery. This perhaps proved to be the most challenging as it was a long process. The first step involved getting an MRI to determine where the problem was in my knee. After the MRI, it was determined that I had a torn meniscus. The second step was to consult the doctor to determine how to correct the problem. It is always a good thing to consult with someone close to you when you receive news that may be disturbing or you don't understand. Keeping it to yourself only increases your anxiety and keeps you worrying about something you can't control.

One of the worst things to do after getting the results about our problems is to do nothing. For some reason, many of us tend to think avoiding our issues will correct the problem, but eventually we must come to the realization that most problems require attention. One of the final steps prior to the surgery was blood work to determine if my heart was strong enough to handle the surgery. It is essential that we check our hearts as well when we experience major changes. It's easy to give the impression that we are okay with the change when we are truly just going through the motions just to appease others. I struggled to make the final decision to have the knee surgery. Although I was reminded of the death of a close friend who recently had knee surgery, I knew that it was the best decision for me.

**THE GREATER THE RISK, THE GREATER THE RETURN**
One of the statements that I never forgot was *the greater the risk, the greater the return*. When I was contemplating knee surgery, I was more concerned with the risk than the return. However, risk and reward is a business concept involving the return on your investment. Higher risk is associated with a greater probability of higher return. On the converse, lower risk is associated with a lower return. In other words, by having knee surgery (the higher risk option), I stood a better chance of returning to my full regiment of working out and exercising. On the other hand, just getting a cortisone shot was lower risk, but there was no guarantee that the shot would ease the pain for more than six months.

Of course, I had the surgery. Shortly thereafter, I began the recovery process. After the second week of recovery and following the doctor's orders to the letter, the initial return was worth the risk that was involved. During this time, I discovered that although the risks were great, following the instructions reduced the risks. For me this was monumental. Here is the thing: most of us seldom read or follow instructions concerning anything because we tend to think we already know what to do and what is expected, which makes us a risk to ourselves. Think about how many of us could have avoided tragedies with our families just by reading someone else's story or following the manual, thereby reducing the risk of falling prey to the same dangers in our lives. The irony with all of this is that the instructions have not changed that much over time. One trusted manual states that it's very simple with regard to the duty of man: "But to do justly, and to love mercy, and to walk humbly with thy God" (Micah 6:8). I think we complicate life when we take it upon ourselves not to adhere to the instructions that have been provided. Experience teaches us that there is a much greater return when we risk a lot, but the joy is in knowing that the risk is actually minimized when we follow the instructions.

**TRUTH MOMENT**
Even though it's all of our hope that we adhere to the doctor's instructions, there are times when you follow the instructions and still get hurt in the process. There are certain injuries that come with the title *man* or *leader*. After serving for almost twenty-five years as a senior pastor, I experienced one of the most devastating things to happen to me as a leader. I had some of my trusted leaders to rise up and accuse me of taking money from the church. It did not matter that I probably had given more than I could ever take with me being the founding pastor and major contributor during its formidable years.

While this is not the first time that any church faced insurrection from within, it was still traumatic for me. It wasn't just that they accused me of the ordeal, but they acted as judge, jury, and executioner. It was not even about me trying to defend myself, but rather being given a chance to speak freely. However, when a person's mind is already made up, nothing you can say or do will change that. Only God can touch the heart of those involved to turn it the way he desires in his time. I have learned that time does not necessarily heal pain and hurt. Only dealing with pain and hurt heals it.

Although many families were hurt, and some left the church, God is faithful. Sometimes when we experience some of our worst battles, God shows up in ways and performs miracles that we never would expect and that only he could perform. During this challenging time, we appointed a youth pastor. Every fourth Sunday it was amazing to see what God was doing through her and her ministry. To help me during this time, I enrolled in seminary in hopes of receiving healing and just to get away from it all. Amazingly, the old saying that what the devil meant for evil, God turns around for good.

Not only did I meet some brothers and sisters that helped walk me through the process of healing, but I also learned one of the greatest lessons as a leader: refuel if you must, but never give up during the heat of the battle. There were days where they just had me laughing the entire time I was in class and other days they just listened as I poured out my heart. Part of our healing often times involves laughter, tears, and just listening to each other's stories. As I walked through my process, I realized that I was not the only person hurting. In fact, all of us in class were at times bleeding while leading. Yet the joy I experienced during the healing process was that I was never alone. One of my professors shared the story about how he was chosen to give the eulogy of one of his mentors and professors and how it was the most challenging thing he had ever done. He further stated that the one thing that got him through the eulogy was seeing the support from so many of his students, colleagues, and friends. The one thing we must remember about the healing process is that there is always someone who has been through, going through, or will go through what we are presently experiencing.

I can recall those days when it was a struggle driving to Richmond for class and listening to the professors' lectures. The battlefield had gotten awfully rough, and there were casualties along the way, but I remember King David when he returned home from battle to find his family and country had been taken, and his men that were on the frontline of the battle with him talked of stoning him. I know firsthand how he felt, but he sought God for his next instructions. The orders he received from God were to pursue and recover all. Although we might not have recovered all yet, I can honestly say we have more now than what we lost. It was not because of me or anyone else, but it was in spite of us; God showed us that he was still in charge. One of the life-changing virtues that I learned during the recovery process was that love is the game changer! We may not like the actions of others or how they treated us, but we still have to love them. We cannot say we love God who we have never seen and hate our brother who we see every day (1 John 4:20).

## Chapter 8

# Accepting Who We Are
### *Stop Trying to Be Like Mike*

I believe it was back in 1991 when the world had become enamored with the Michael Jordan theme *Be Like Mike*. Although it was a Gatorade® commercial promoting their energy drink, the *Be Like Mike* theme took off around the world, and Michael Jordan became a household name. From the Jordan® sneakers to young men sticking their tongue out while playing basketball, all were trying to imitate the *Be Like Mike* theme. However, sometimes what is lost in the process of trying to be like someone else, is we stop accepting who we are. The challenge, however, is how do we accept who we are when we don't know who we are . . . how do we accept who we are when we don't want to be who we are? Although it appears that there are more questions than answers, the fact remains, we must find a way to accept who we are in spite of what we may have encountered in life.

I recall facing a crisis with my identity when I was in middle school. My older brother had just encountered a tragedy when he was jumped by several guys at a neighborhood playground. Because he was beaten by the guys, my brother went home and later returned with a knife stabbing and killing one of the young men who jumped him. It happened on a Sunday afternoon while I was out of town with my grandmother attending a church service. When we returned home later that evening and saw all of the police cars in front of our door, we were frightened to say the least. Even after sorting through all the details from the tragedy that day, I never got a chance to talk to my brother. Because of the nature of this incident, my siblings and I stayed out of school for several weeks.

Upon returning to school, I totally removed myself from any interaction with other students to avoid answering any questions. The incident also strained the relationship with one of my best friends because he was the cousin of the young man who had been killed. I told my teacher that I did not want to be at school. When my teacher inquired further as to what was wrong with me, I explained to her the situation and that I was scared to be at school. I was in the seventh grade at the time, and from that point on I began to live in fear of something happening to me. Although I did not realize it at the time, fear was slowly trying to rob me of who I was in life.

I started questioning why things happened and why did my brother have to go through this tragedy at such a young age. Fear can be a crippling force if it goes unchecked too long. The more I became afraid of what may happen at school, the more I began to hate who I was as a person. It was not that someone was threatening me at school, but it was the fear that something may happen to me. So often we live our lives based on the *what if* instead of the *what is*. When we live this way, we lose the possibilities of experiencing a greater tomorrow.

## Fear is a Game Changer

By walking in fear, not only do we run the risk of not fulfilling our destiny, but we also allow fear to change our game and who we are in light of who we were created to be. While it's okay to want to *Be Like Mike*, at some point in our lives we have to embrace who we are and stop being afraid of what others may think. The real reason why I was afraid to go to school was because of what I thought others were saying about me because of the tragedy.

Fear has a way of camouflaging the real issue. It causes us to try to hide who we are because of what we have been through. In my case, fear almost changed my game. I did not want to be who I was created to be because of what happened in my life. There will always be some challenging events, circumstances, and situations that will happen with all of us, but we cannot allow the events to change who we are.

## Be the Best Version of You

So, instead of us trying to *Be Like Mike* or anyone else, just be the best version of you. Nobody can be better at being you than you. The challenge is accepting who we are and then finding ways to be better at it. During the time I was still coaching, I recall a young man coming up to me after a game we had just won. The young man said, "Coach Thornhill, I want to be a coach like you. I watched you on the sideline and your cool and calm demeanor really inspired me to be like you." While I was extremely humbled by the young man and him wanting to be a coach especially like me, I quickly told him it's more to it than looking good. We often get a visual from what's on television or what we see in person, but never know what goes on behind the scenes. The coach he saw that was calm and collected that night on the sideline is not always that way. I wanted to tell him if he came to one of our practices during the week and saw me then, maybe he would not want to be like me or even a coach for that matter.

Sometimes we only see the good version or good side of the person that we want to be like and never see the other side. Consequently, we short change ourselves and others because we only see *the head side* of the coin and not the *tail side*. In order to see both sides, we have to be willing to flip the coin by going to practice and other events to see the true person, not just their demeanor at game time.

Most of the time, we all perform well at the game; however, it's when nobody is observing, and we are in closed practices that we find out if we really want to *be like Mike*. After I invited the young man to one of our practices so he could see how we operate as a team and how the players carry themselves, he said maybe he would reconsider being a coach. How many times have we all missed certain opportunities such as teaching, being a counselor, or an administrator because we made a decision to be something or do something, only to find out that what we saw the first time was not what happens all the time? I wanted to teach when I first graduated but I did not think I would like creating lesson plans each week. I later found out that preparing lesson plans was not all that bad if you were a good teacher. Instead of wanting or trying to be like someone else, learn the art of being the best you that you can possibly be. This starts with you looking into the mirror each day and saying "There is no one better at being me than me." If, by chance, someone suggests they want to be like you, just let them know that your number has already been taken ... by you.

### Closing the Door on Missed Opportunities

When we look back over the years, we may have a tendency to fuss over *spilt milk*, but we must also learn to close certain doors that have been open too long. It does no good to get upset over a bad decision or unfortunate event that has already come to pass and cannot be changed. I used to spend a lot of time thinking about what I could have done differently during the time my church went through the split. However, I soon realized that if I did not close the door on that chapter of my life, it would prevent me from experiencing the upcoming chapters which would ultimately cement my legacy.

As most of us know, some doors will never open for us until we learn to close other doors that drain us of who we are and could be. If we were to take a closer look, many of us would find that some doors that we thought were missed opportunities were blessings in disguise. On one occasion, I thought I had missed a great opportunity to buy a used vehicle during my sophomore year in high school. I told my dad the car was only $600 dollars, and if I did not get it that day, someone else would buy it. Needless to say, my dad did not buy the car because he said I did not need a car at that time. Later that month, I saw the guy who bought the car and he was sorry that he purchased it. Not only was there too much work to be done to the car, it was also a gas guzzler. The young man further stated he was trying to sell the car because he could not afford the gas. Of course, I was smiling, and later thanked my father for not allowing me to get the car.

It's almost similar to our heavenly Father. Sometimes he doesn't allow us to get things or do things in an effort to protect us from ourselves. As we get older and we look back over certain parts of our lives, we then appreciate the fact that we were protected from things that could have injured or perhaps killed us earlier. I could not override my dad to purchase the car. However, when our heavenly Father constantly tells us no and we go out anyway to do what we want simply because we know that we can, it's a recipe for disaster.

I know some of us think that experience is the best teacher. Well I would argue that it is actually the most costly teacher. I believe listening to and following someone else's experiences is the best teacher. Why go through hell when you don't have to, just to say you have the experience.

**TRUTH MOMENT**
Over the last few years I have become more reflective with respect to legacy, my impact on this current generation, and our ever-changing culture. I learned a great lesson from one of my professors while in school. He said that if we are going to ever change things around us, we must be in a position to change the policy. People will listen to you all day but continue to do what they have always done because that is what the policy allows. To be a game changer, you have to get involved in the game and then be willing to change certain polices. It has been said that a rising tide causes all ships to sail, but if you don't have access to the water you are still at square one.

Fortunately, I had the opportunity to get involved in the game, and as a result, I'm proud to say some changes were made. Serving on several boards in my community, I made it clear to my constituents and fellow board members that I was not there to be liked, but to make a difference. As a member of a local board, we were faced with one of the toughest decisions at that time. The decision involved renewing the contract of the executive director or releasing him and going in a different direction. After much discussion and thought, we decided to go in a different direction. As the chair of the board, I had to lead the other members in a decision that would set the course for the future and the entire region. Needless to say, it turned out to be the best decision for the entire region. It not only changed the entire culture of the agency, but the morale changed overnight. Many were thanking the board after the decision because it charted a new course not just for today but for the future. I share this moment because in our decision making, we cannot allow fear to drive us to where we can only see things today. We must be bold and courageous enough to look at the bigger picture in hopes of making a better tomorrow for us all. Fear may be a game changer, but never allow it to change who you are.

## Chapter 9
# Taking Risks
*It's Part of the Process*

I think the one thing that perhaps defines who I am as a pastor, coach, educator, community leader, and now author, are the words *risk taker*. Now I know to the church folks, taking risks is nothing new, for we walk by faith and not by sight. To the business person, taking risks is essentially walking by faith and not by sight. Although the risks are great, the potential returns make it all worth the struggle. For the sake of this chapter, we will use the term risk and faith interchangeably. According to the writer of the book of Hebrews, without faith it is impossible to please God (Hebrews 11:6).

Said a different way in the business world, the greater the risk the greater the return. If we are ever going to accomplish anything of value or lasting reward, we must be willing to launch out into the deep and leave our comfort zones. When I started the church that I have now been pastoring for over twenty-five years, I left the comfort of a four-bedroom home in Chesterfield County, Virginia and moved to a one-bedroom house in Lawrenceville, Virginia, shared with an older lady, who was well over eighty years old at the time. To some it may not have made sense, but those of us who are risk takers and faith walkers understand the journey. Although I did not move my family down right away, they would eventually come after several months. Sometimes in our journey to locating our destiny, we have to be willing go where no one would go. It's simply not enough to read and talk about Abraham leaving everything and everyone, but then we start stammering when it's our time to walk by faith (Genesis 12: 1). I'm not suggesting that we make a decision like that without consulting God or someone you trust, but when it's time to move we have to move.

### Risk Takers See the End From the Beginning

Even though some folks said I was crazy to leave a job with great benefits and a home in the suburbs, I knew deep down that God had something better for me. It was not just about leaving the job and my home, but I knew that God's benefit package was much better than the State of Virginia could ever offer. Most people look at the salary package and will generally take a job because of the pay, but I have always said it's not the pay that makes the job but it's the benefit package. In this case, the pay nor benefit package looked inviting when it came down to moving to rural Brunswick County. However, since I was a risk taker, I believed I got a visual of the end from the beginning. I saw a school, mentoring program for young men, a youth basketball program, and a church that would be on the cutting edge of 21st century ministry.

While all of this was a dream to some, I could see it as a reality. One of the first things we did after establishing the church was to have a summer basketball league. All I had was an idea and the faith to believe that it would all work out.

Initially, this was a stretch because there were no outdoor facilities to accommodate the league. However, stepping out in faith again, I sought the school board's permission to use one of their outdoor facilities. I also agreed to upgrade the facility by providing asphalt to redo the surface of the court. To show you how the Lord works when you step out in faith, all of the asphalt, the trucks to deliver the asphalt, and the company to pave the court was donated.

This all had to be completed in about two weeks because school was soon to end for the year and summer was around the corner. Everything fell into place: the courts were resurfaced, the teams were selected, and the officials were in place as we started our first summer basketball league! On that first night, over ten teams participated and over 200 fans were in attendance to watch some good old "black top" basketball. We played two nights a week and it gave the kids and community something to do during the summer.

Sometimes we never know the impact that our lives will have on others when we are willing to make sacrifices and do something that others may be afraid of doing. Although I had no intentions of moving to Brunswick County to establish a church, taking the risk to do something outside of the norms reaped benefits far greater than I ever thought. When we are willing to give of our resources and our talents, we never know when we may need similar things from others as we get older.

Just recently my son worked for several months on a temporary job because it was difficult finding a regular job due to his previous record for driving under the influence. Prior to him getting the job, I talked with the employer who remembered me working with so many young people during the summer. After talking with him, he stated that he would hire my son on a temporary basis, not because of his experience, but because of my experience. This startled me because my son had never worked before in that capacity as a temporary employee, especially with the county government. This may seem like a small thing to some, but there is truth to the statement "whatsoever a man soweth that shall he also reap" (Galatians 6:7). In other words, what we do for others will eventually come back to us. The time I spent counseling, teaching, and training young men was not in vain. Never think that helping, training, developing, and mentoring others is a waste of time. Just when we least expect it, the tables have a way of turning around on our behalf. Someone in your family may be the beneficiary of a simple act of kindness that was done by you years earlier. Don't be afraid to launch out into the deep; you may just reel in something much bigger than you expected.

### Know When to Pass the Baton

At that time, I was the founder, director, and head person of the league. However, after a few years, I passed the baton and let some other young men carry it further. As excited as I was in getting the summer basketball league established, I knew I could not continue if I wanted to see other ventures established in this rural area. As I mentioned in an earlier chapter, if we ever want to see growth in any organization or endeavor, we must be willing to pass the baton to others. Passing the baton allows others to bring something fresh and innovative to the table.

One of the tragedies of leaders is the fear of allowing others to take our place. We think we are no longer useful when it's time to pass the baton, but we can never really fulfill all the Lord has in store for us unless we are willing to move or change from our present location. As I previously stated, I moved from Richmond, Virginia to Lawrenceville, Virginia over twenty-five years ago. I have grown and learned so much about rural America. As much as I have learned by relocating to Lawrenceville, I know that this is not my final destination. I know when the time is right I will be relocating again, hopefully to Charlotte, North Carolina. Refusing to move often stifles our growth and the growth of the organization. Those who fail to understand this principle will either be lost in the process or die along the way. The death is usually due to failure to see "another train coming" after being warned. It is similar to technology—those who did not see the world wide web and the internet coming are now lost. Those companies who failed to make the needed updates and continuous transitions are dying if not already dead.

For some it's hard to pass the baton because it's the only thing they have done. But that is even more of a reason to pass it if we are to keep up with the changes that come every day. When we have not been exposed to anything other than what we have been doing, we almost always become obsolete and run the risk of being shut down by default. After I passed the baton on to someone else, it allowed me to focus my energies on establishing a mentoring program that would assist young men aspiring for excellence in education and developing better work ethics.

### Real Outreach is One Person at a Time

Some may be wondering when I was planning on establishing outreach for the church and building the membership. Believe it not, the basketball league was my outreach and the mentoring program was my discipleship program. My belief was that if people would see who I was everyday on the basketball court, they would not have any problem with coming to see what I had to say on Sunday morning.

Quite to my surprise, one of the toughest and most difficult persons that I had to deal with during my summer league became one of my most avid supporters and followers. Although he no longer lives in the area, he gave me a hammer for Father's Day. Inscribed on the hammer was, "Thanks Preacher Man for helping me build my life." This was the best gift I could have ever received, and I keep it on my desk to remind me each day that ministry is one person at a time. We never know whose life we are building when we do the little things and do what the Lord puts in our hearts to do. It may not be what others are doing, but as long as it's reaching the lost at any cost, then it's ministry. I don't know if it was the basketball league or the mentoring program, but all I know is that he got the message.

Jesus told stories from farmers and seeds to a man who was left for dead by robbers, and he reached the masses. If we can reach a few by taking the gospel to the black top or mentoring young men who don't have fathers in their lives, then to God be the glory! At the end of day, the hope is that we have done the work of our Father and some person's life has changed as a result of the gospel message that was preached or demonstrated. There are converts we will never know we touched simply because we might inspire one's growth. One plants when he introduces the gospel message to the person. Another waters when he encourages and further explains the gospel message to the person. However, at the end of the day, it is only God who can give the increase or help that person to grow.

Some of the increase may be what we see every Sunday and at church, but the other increase may have been a fan who was watching the game or a police officer who was passing by the game. At any rate, we must not be disappointed if we don't see the immediate results on Sunday morning. I did not see the fruits of our labor until years later when the college students visited the church for homecoming or some other special event. When they testifyied how the mentoring program during the school year made a significant difference in their walk with Christ, it blessed me and all those who had come years after the church had been established.

**TRUTH MOMENT**

As exciting as it was during the summer with the basketball league and the mentoring program, we still struggled with a small membership. It was during that time that I launched out in faith again by establishing a live radio broadcast every Sunday. As if I needed another venture to start, I'm sure the residents of Brunswick and Mecklenburg Counties were thinking, *That is a very energetic young man.* What they did not know at the time was that prior to coming to Lawrenceville, I did have some radio experience while I served at my home church in Richmond. I started the broadcast in Brunswick, and did it live for five years. However, with technology evolving each year, I soon went from live broadcasting to sending a pre-recorded message each week. Although they were pre-recorded messages, the response to the broadcast was great which caused an influx of visitors to come on Sundays.

On one occasion when I went to another church to preach, I had a young man come up to me afterwards and say, "I listen to you every Sunday morning, but I thought you were a tall man." I laughed and said, "Why did you think that?" He further stated that it was just how he pictured me. It's amazing how we are viewed by some who never had the opportunity to lay eyes upon us. How many times do we form preconceived ideas and images of people whom we have never seen or had the opportunity to meet? How many times do we miss the opportunity to witness or share our story with others because of how we think they might view us or worse, how we view them? As coaches often say after viewing the film and scouting report of an opposing team, the game still has to be played between the lines. Such as it is in ministry: the gospel still has to be shared in order to be heard.

## Chapter 10
# Igniting the Fire
*You Were Made in His Image, So Go For It*

One of the most difficult things to do in almost anything is getting started. Writing this book has been in me for a while, but igniting the fire to get it going was a task. For starters, it was about seven years ago while I was completing my seminary work at Virginia Union University that the thought of writing a book was birthed in my heart. I was talking to one of my colleagues and I was sharing with him the struggles I encountered when I began seminary and the joy I felt as I prepared to graduate. It then struck me that I needed to recapture the moments in a book with the hope of helping other leaders who may experience similar battles in ministry and life. While I was excited to share the news with my colleague about possibly writing a book, I soon lost the drive when I started the coursework toward my doctorate immediately after I graduated from seminary.

So, for three to four years during the time I was completing my doctorate, I had more thoughts of writing the book, especially while I was working on my dissertation. There were nights of complete frustration where I said to myself, *If writing my dissertation is this tough, I should have just written the book.* After three and a half years of course work and completing my dissertation, I revisited the idea of writing a book. Because I was so exhausted from the dissertation process, I convinced myself to take a year off just to rest. However, a year turned into two and before you knew it, three years had passed, and writing the book became a distant memory until I happened to see that same colleague who graduated from seminary with me.

As we were talking, he asked what I planned on doing for the next few years. I responded by saying possibly retire and move to Charlotte, North Carolina. He then asked, "What about that book you said you were going to write?" He caught me off guard and I simply responded, "I will get to it soon." Truthfully, I was tired and had lost the drive to write the book. For many of us, we have the desire to do a lot of things, but often we get side tracked by the daily struggles in life. It was in me to write but I needed something to ignite the fire.

As the days would pass, I begin to experience pain in my knee from a previous automobile accident. After several visits to the doctor, he referred me to an orthopedic specialist. The test results indicated that I had a torn meniscus. The specialist gave me three options: a cortisone shot, physical therapy, or knee surgery. Because I did not want a temporary fix with a cortisone shot, I opted for knee surgery which would provide lasting results from a meniscus repair.

After reading a pamphlet from the doctor's office about arthroscopic knee surgery and how it's performed, something really ignited in me about writing the book again. It was like my mojo had returned after reading the pamphlet. As I read how the surgeon had to take a scope to look behind the knee to correct the meniscus tear, I began to think about other *tears* in our lives that can only be seen and corrected by the master surgeon. I further began to think about some *emotional tears* in my life with my son, daughter, and my wife that have been covered for so long and needed to be corrected. I also started thinking about *tears* in my life when I was growing up in the city of Richmond trying to survive on the playgrounds while playing basketball. My mind then went back to the time when my brother was attacked and beaten by a group of guys on that same playground and then came back and killed one of the guys who attacked him. So, deciding to undergo knee surgery became the kiln wood that reignited the fire in me to write the book. For some reason a litany of my past tragedies flashed before me and this is when I knew *Menspiration* had to manifest.

Although the book was in me for many years, and my knee surgery became the impetus to get me started, it was still a process getting through each chapter. It seemed like an eternity to get it done. I had my good days where my thoughts would flow and then there were those days where I experienced writer's block and could not write anything. It was frustrating and tempting to give up, but I would simply step away from it for several days and then start back again. Many times, we start the race well without thinking about the bumps and potholes we may encounter on the road to success. But it's during those times that we have to dig deep and push forward with determination and discipline to get it done.

In my case, I pushed forward by talking to those who supported me throughout the process. Also, I talked with other authors about how to cope with days when your creative juices just don't flow. Just to hear them say, "We all have those days," meant the world to me. Since I am the type of person who likes to get things done in a timely fashion, it was extremely rough when some days turned into weeks with little or no writing to show for my efforts. However, I got through those days by doing something else that I enjoyed such as watching a game on television or just going to the movie. The key for me was taking a small break so that I could refresh my mind and thoughts. After doing so, I was able to get back into the flow of writing and eventually had a complete manuscript. It took six months for me to complete the manuscript; six months of patience, persistence, and perseverance. I needed patience to stay with it even during times when I really felt like putting it off for another two or three years until I retired. Persistence was key on the days I was distracted and wanted to do other activities. Finally, it took much persevering in spite of the difficulties, obstacles, and discouragement along the way.

### Keep Fanning the Flame

I know this may sound somewhat elementary, but my hope is that as you walk slowly with me through this process, your book, your business, and your dream will start to come into focus. Igniting the fire is great, but keeping the fire going is just as important. I was given a four- to six-week recovery window from my knee surgery. My goal was to write a chapter each day and be free from distractions. The television, phone, and visitors were all possible distractions. Being a pastor and community leader comes with a lot of duties and responsibilities. Not to mention I just had surgery, so I couldn't turn off my phone in the event my wife or someone else called to check on me regarding an emergency or something involving the church.

However, that four to six weeks window of possibly completing the book turned into six months. Writing a chapter a day turned into a chapter every two to three weeks. As I look back, not only was my original timeline unrealistic, but trying to condense the burning fire of wanting to write five to seven years ago into four to six weeks was virtually impossible. There were days I experienced writer's block, days

I could not recall past chapters in my life, and other days I simply was not focused. These were significant challenges. For some it may be easy to ignite the flame, but keeping it burning is often difficult and demanding. All these things happened, but what kept me writing was knowing that I was too close and being confident I could get it done.

This reminded me of the time I played sports in high school. Preseason training was always a difficult time for everyone. To get in shape, the first few weeks were spent building up your stamina so that you could endure the long season ahead. One of the worst things as an athlete is to start the season strong, but not be able to finish due to poor physical conditioning and lack of endurance. Some of the preseason training including long distance running, wind sprints, and other exercises to increase the oxygen in your lungs. When the oxygen is increased in your lungs you usually can endure the strenuous activities on the field or court while you are playing the game.

As a former athlete, the discipline that I gained from my earlier days helped me during the writing process. There were days during preseason workouts I wanted to quit as I was gasping for air, but eventually my "second wind kicked in" and I recovered. A second wind is a new surge of energy after a period of mental or physical exhaustion. It also refers to our metabolism changes to a more efficient mode during prolonged exercise. There were similar days at the computer that I felt like I was gasping for air but thank God for my second wind. It was a long process, however, I survived and got it done.

### Finishing What We Start

As I thought about finishing this book, I was reminded that the race is not to the swift neither the battle to the strong but to him that endures to the end. Sometimes to complete what we start, it requires discipline, desire, and determination. I knew I had the desire and the determination, but the discipline was at times fading, especially when visitors would come by or the phone was ringing. At the end of the day, if you want to keep the fire burning or complete what you started, there aren't always easy answers. As men we sometimes look for an alternate route to doing something, or we give a legitimate reason for not being what we should be or could be, but the fact remains, it's on us and we are ultimately responsible. We can have a well-defined game plan, as I did, and we can have good intentions of finishing what we started, but we are judged on the final results. If the results are incomplete, then our followers will see it that way as well.

It may sound hard but that is why we need other men in our lives to walk us through the process and at the same time be transparent enough to show us where they failed. Down through the years, I failed at spending quality time with my son and daughter. When I should have been doing things with them I was helping others. However, I did ask my son and daughter to forgive me for missing the mark with them. Although we can never turn back the hand of time, we can change the future by acknowledging our mistakes in the present. By doing so, I can begin to make changes in my behavior and hope that my children are able to move forward with less baggage in their lives.

I don't claim to be a prolific writer or scholar, quite the contrary; but I do know that recovery is much easier when you follow instructions and when you listen to someone who has been where you are going. Much of who I am and what I do is because of my passion to help other men through their struggles. Moreover, it has to do with the wisdom I obtained from listening to older men and just reading.

**TRUTH MOMENT**
I know there are at least five to ten projects I started and stopped over the course of my life. However, there is one project that I started and I'm still at it twenty-five years lat-

er—pastoring. Yes, I came out the gate running and on fire. There were times where circumstances, events, and struggles caused me to slow down, but my fire never burned out. I believe that sometimes others do not realize that our fire is still burning because they only see us from a distance. What almost caused my fire to fizzle out was being overly concerned with those who could not see that the coals were still burning and simply needed to be turned over. There were times where I wanted to turn the coals over but was simply too weak.

Just when it looked like it was over, I was rejuvenated by a word from an unlikely individual. One evening I was sitting on the back of my truck and a gentleman that I did not know came by. He said he was just passing by and saw my truck in the parking lot. What he did not know was that I had just finished crying because I felt abandoned by those who I had trusted. The gentleman simply said, "Pastor Thornhill, I thank God for your ministry." That was it and he left. From that time until now I know that weeping may endure for a night, but joy comes in the morning. Although it was still evening and the sun was beginning to set, I knew God had sent the man to me just to let me know that better days were ahead. Sometimes when we are at our lowest and nobody knows the weight we are carrying, God will always send us what we need, who we need, and when we need it. In a very real way, he will be our refuge and strength, a very present help in the time of trouble. I was in real trouble and he sent help!

Maybe you are in trouble now . . . Let's pray.

Father, we thank you for being an all sufficient God. You know our ending from the beginning, so whatever my brother or sister may be encountering or experiencing, touch, heal, and deliver them. Let them know there is nothing you cannot handle and that you are a very present help in their trouble. We thank you that it is already done. In Jesus' name we pray, AMEN!

CHAPTER 11

# Owning your Destiny
*Don't Let No One Hijack Your Story*

Life can sometimes take its twists, turns, and even pitfalls, but at the end of the journey, we still have to give an account of what we did or did not do in this life. We have to own our destiny, good or bad. Contrary to what some may say, I believe you make your own destiny and we tweak it every day. However, at times there are certain events that may influence our destiny but ultimately, we control it. I also believe we are born with certain gifts and talents, but they don't just work by themselves, we guide them.

I know that I was born with the gift of gab and oratorical skills, but if never used, they are just skills that lie dormant. There are times where we may have the opportunity to exercise our gifts but decide not to just because others discourage us from using them. In some cases, we are discouraged by these individuals when they may be coveting or jealous of your gift. But we can never allow others to stop us from doing something we were created to do, even when we feel that others may be able to do it better. It's during those times that we hone our skills and get better at perfecting our gifts.

I remember as early as the fifth grade that I had a knack for public speaking. However, it was not until I was in high school that I started using it. On one occasion I was asked by a teacher to speak on behalf of all the athletes in school and express my feelings on some changes that needed to be made. It went so well that other schools in our district asked me to represent them as well.

Sometimes when you are trying to do well, evil is always present. There were a group of students who had become jealous because of the number of requests I was receiving. To make matters worse, one of my closest friends was leading the assault. They were trying to hijack my destiny as a speaker and make me feel bad in the process which made me extremely upset. However, after thinking it through, I still accepted the speaking requests. I also talked to my friend away from the others to let him know that I was more hurt than I was upset about what happened. As it turned out, my friend believed he was gifted to speak and wanted to speak as well. He even thought I was soliciting the speaking engagements. I told him that if he really wanted to speak, we could tag team.

On the day of the event that we agreed to speak together, he became nervous and could not speak. As a result, I spoke on his behalf. Not only did he thank me, but he told our other friends that I was the best friend he had. Sometimes when others think they can do what you are called to do, give them the opportunity and see what happens. They may soon find out that looks are deceiving; some things are harder than they appear to be.

However, after this incident, I stopped speaking all together at special events. I would defer to others by suggesting that I was hoarse and could not speak anyway. A teacher found out what I was doing and called me into her classroom. She explained to me that I cannot apologize for being a gifted speaker and that if people had a problem with it, then it was their problem. She further stated that if I let people dictate to me now regarding my gift and where I could possibly go in life, I would regret it. That conversation set a new course for my life. From that time on, I accepted every opportunity to speak. Some of the same individuals that I thought were my friends disappeared. Initially, it was a tough pill to swallow. However, I soon realized that they were simply trying to hijack my destiny. Since they could not speak well, they did not want me to speak at all.

As I progressed through school and life, I was careful to own my destiny. Nothing became clearer to me than this fact: nobody can stop my destiny or path in life other than me. My destiny can only be stopped by S.I.N.: self-inflicted nonsense. The only other way is if I choose to relinquish it because of fear—the fear of what they think about me or what they have to say about me. Owning my destiny does not mean I try to deny or escape certain events that may have happened in my life. It means I own the mistake, but mistakes do not own me. I take responsibility for my actions and repent if I was wrong. I make no apologies for the success I may be experiencing. I share my story as many times as possible with as many people as possible, so that others know that what may seem impossible is not only possible but can lead to great success. Also, when we share our stories it just may be the antidote to help someone out of a tragic encounter in their life. In owning my destiny, my story is unique; therefore, no one can hijack it just by repeating everything I do or say. We all have our own story, and no one can tell it or write about unless we share it.

By sharing our story with other men, we can ensure success while mentoring and helping all of us to finish strong. In partnering with other men, it involves being accountable by at least having two other men in your life. I refer to this as the "Abraham and Timothy principle." Abraham in the biblical sense was considered to be the father of faith (Romans 4:16). Therefore, we all need a father figure that we can look up to and consult with during critical and crucial times in life. Particularly, when we may be struggling with trust issues at home, on our job, or just in general. The idea is not to try to carry it alone but to seek the counsel of others who have been in similar situations. Solomon said it best: "A person standing alone can be attacked and defeated, but two can stand back to back and conquer. Three are even better for a triple-braided cord is not easily broken" (Ecclesiastes 4:12 NLT).

On the other hand, the Timothy principle is the opposite—we need sons to "pour into" so that they can continue the legacy of the fathers. Timothy was a son of his spiritual father Paul and he left these words with Timothy, "You have heard me teach things that have been confirmed by many reliable witnesses. Now teach these truths to other trustworthy people who will be able to pass them on to others" (2 Timothy 2:2 NLT). When we pour into others, we pass on vital information to younger men to ensure their success and to help them avoid similar mistakes we've made. Noted author Myles Munroe shared the story of a dying father leaving everything to one of three sons because that son loved him and always sought the counsel of his father in critical times.[7] The story suggested that it is not always the smartest person or oldest that get the spoils, but the one who listened and responded to the heart of the father. We all need sons to "pour into" for succession purposes.

Mentoring is another component of menspiration to inspire men to conquer life's mountains. It involves coaching and guiding others through tragedies, disappointment and simply daily struggles. This means we cannot hold onto the knowledge, experience, achievements, opportunities, or relationships we accrue in our positions. We must be willing to share this information with our mentees in hopes of them gaining experience along the way and becoming motivated to pass it on to other men. In doing so the legacy and destiny of not only a few are shaped, but of generations.

Finally, my hope is that we can all finish strong. Finishing has more to do with staying connected to a host of men rather than trying to do things alone. When we disconnect from others we open ourselves up to becoming easy targets and, in some cases, ending up as a casualty. It reminded me of the parable that Jesus told about the vine and branches, he stated, "I am the vine; you are the branches. If you remain in me and I in you, you will bear much fruit; apart from me you can do nothing" (John 15:5). When we are connected, we draw strength from others and in the process, we grow, mature and fulfill our destiny as leaders.

## Paving the Way for Others to Follow

Although destiny is about us, legacy is about what we leave to others. Now that we have secured our destiny, it is important that we pave the way for others to follow. Over the last few years of ministry, I have spent more time on succession rather than progression. This is not to suggest that progress is any less important, but if we don't have a succession plan ministry dies with us. The late Myles Munroe said it best: "You cannot have succession without a successor."[8] If we want the vision to live longer than the man, we must find a way to promote the idea of a successor. I have seen ministries, organizations, and affiliations die because of the lack of a succession plan. The fact remains, no matter how great we are as leaders, we all have an appointment with death, some sooner and others later. Therefore, the better we prepare our successor, the longer the vision lasts.

King Solomon said where there is no vision the people will perish (Proverbs 29:18). I say where there is no successor the vision will parish. Even though having a succession plan in place does not guarantee a smooth transition in leadership, not having one almost guarantees the opposite. I witnessed an organization not having one in place and it almost split the organization. The lack of transparency and failure to train other young men and women for leadership is simply a recipe for disaster.

When leaders only share their intentions regarding succession with one or two individuals instead of sharing it with the entire leadership team, it creates division among leaders. It's not that the other leaders cannot handle sensitive information, but you create an environment that shows you don't trust them enough to share the information with them. In addition, it creates factions when those who have served and been with the leader for years receive sensitive information from sources outside of the leadership team. We often see it in Third World Countries when a leader dies and there is no one in place, there is almost an undermining that immediately occurs to overthrow the existing government. So, it's not a possibility that something like this is going to happen, but almost a guarantee. The idiom "power corrupts, and absolute power corrupts absolutely" is actually seen in situations without a succession plan.

Creating the legs for our legacy is just as important as securing and owning our destiny. Even though you cannot have one without the other, it's equally important that planning be a part of the process. Over the last few years that I have been teaching this subject, I have seen more men come to grips with their mortality and spending the time to share with other men. As men it's not always easy to be transparent with other men even though we are more alike than different. We hurt, we cry, and we make mistakes, but we all want the best for our families. To continue to pave the way for others to follow, we must be intentional, transparent, and willing to share our story.

## It's Not Easy to Open the Door

In sharing our story, it's not always easy to open the door when you have been hurt. One of the hardest things for me to do after encountering betrayal was to trust again. It was not that I did not want to trust again, it was simply a struggle to open the door fully to let anyone in. My wife helped me to understand this completely. After she explained to me how she felt when I betrayed her trust, I then understood. The hurt, anger, and resentment just does not go away overnight. In many cases, counseling is the only thing that helps you to deal with it, and you still have those days where it's a struggle. Sometimes the effect of betrayal is deeper than we realize. Consequently, if it is not harnessed and checked, it can hinder all of your relationships. We then began to view all relationships through the window of those who hurt us, and we never give ourselves a chance to heal because we continue to nurse our pain, rehearse our pain, and at times, curse our pain.

When we do this, we never give the Lord a chance to reverse our pain and help us move forward. By no means am I suggesting that the recovery process happens overnight, but I am saying we have to start somewhere. Usually, the starting point is with yourself and not others. I believe if we can agree to be honest with ourselves then we can move forward. *Menspiration* is about helping men to open the door of communication to talk about the hurt, while also moving to and through the recovery process. The emphasis here is on the word *process*, a series of actions and steps where we are intentional about our feelings and concerns with the hope of healing and recovery at the end.

Sometimes when we are not clear about our intended actions, we assume that others understand where we are coming from. In the case of opening the door to our story, we do not always let people in because they want more than we are willing to give at the time. For me, the hurt did subside, but I only let those in who had a relationship with me. I remember telling my wife for my 50th birthday celebration, I did not want people there who had hurt me. This was no slight towards anyone, but I was simply being honest. I did not want to fake a smile with someone when I was still reeling from the pain they inflicted. I believe one of the worst things we can do is pretend with someone when the pain from the wound is still fresh. The beauty, however, is that I was able to live through it, recover from it, and now share it. There's no benefit to have gone through a storm and not be willing to share it with someone else to help them through theirs as well.

**TRUTH MOMENT**
Although destiny and legacy come as a package deal, sometimes we want one at the expense of the other. I remember sharing with my son when he got into some trouble his junior year in college, and I would always tell him don't forfeit your destiny. One summer I was called by my son's coach to come to Charlotte, NC because he had gotten into some trouble. To make matters worse, this was my first day back at school and we were in training with all the teachers. When I arrived in Charlotte, I told him no matter what he got involved in, his destiny is what he makes it, not by following others. I also told him regardless of what others do or say, he is responsible for his own actions. If he wanted to abort his destiny by getting involved in stuff he knew was not beneficial, he would regret it.

My son did not take my advice, and he got into more trouble. Unfortunately, the consequences were severe, and his destiny was altered. It hurt me to see him suffer during this period of his life where he wished he had listened; however, the situation did end up saving his life in the long run. Although he could not drive for almost five years, he realized that it could have been much worse. Sometimes our destiny is altered due to our own mistakes and the failure to listen to those who are part of the process. It's amazing when he and I talk now, we reflect back to some of things I shared with him while he was in high school. He wished that he had listened back then, maybe he would not have gone through as much as he did and be further along than where he is now. The irony is that he did not know back then what he knows now, but if he did know, perhaps he would not have experienced what he did several years ago.

I stated in an earlier chapter that experience is not always the best teacher, but a costly teacher. The best teacher is listening and learning from the mistakes of others, so you do not have to experience them yourself. I'm sure my son could speak to this subject in detail. Although he is back to driving and coaching himself, we both joke about learning things the hard way. Now, some of our best times together are when we go fishing; there are no interruptions or distractions because you cannot get a signal on your phone when you are in the middle of the Atlantic Ocean. In fact, he constantly shares with me some of the things he talks with his players about that were very similar to what I shared with him and my players. Even though the consequences of his actions halted his destiny, the joy I have as a father is that he did learn.

CHAPTER 12

# Never Say Never
*Who Knows, This May Be Your Time*

I'm sure we have said these things at one time or another: I will never go to that place again, I will never let them do it again, or I will never be that kind of person. At some point, we were either upset, disappointed, or angry enough that we made these rash statements. The truth is that none of us know when purpose and destiny may collide at a street called *divine appointment* and we may be forced to eat those words.

I remember on several occasions when I said those very words. The first occasion was growing up in the church and listening to different ministers who believed the need to go to seminary for training was a waste of time. At the time, I said I would never go to seminary. I heard all the jokes some would say like: you mean cemetery not seminary. To make matters worse, my former pastor frowned upon the idea and alluded to the same jokes. Later on in life and after finishing undergraduate school at Virginia Commonwealth University, my brother decided to go to seminary because he was going through some transitions in his life. He not only attended, but he even brought back a lot of the teaching to our former church. My former pastor not only frowned at his teachings from the seminary, but she even "threw shade" at him during her Bible studies and Sunday morning messages. My grandmother, who was the assistant pastor at the time, did not think too much of it either. She would always use the phrase, "The letter killeth, but the spirit giveth life" (1 Corinthians 3:6). She would use this verse from the Bible to discourage the young ministers from attending school to receive formal training to preach. After not being able to deal with the constant ridicule, my brother made the decision to leave our home church and attend another church. I later found out that seminary not only helped him spiritually, but it was therapeutic for him during the transition he was experiencing.

After a while, I eventually left my home church and began attending the same church as my brother. We were considered by some as the *dynamic duo* because we both became associate ministers at that church and would often host a daily radio program along with the senior pastor. At one point, the three of us would *pinch hit* or stand in for the other. Amazingly, some of the people that listened to the radio broadcast could not tell us apart. At any rate, my brother would later move to take over another church as pastor and I would later move to begin my own church in Lawrenceville, VA.

### Don't Let Others Write Your Story

About eight years after I had been pastoring, the church went through a split that almost sent me back home to Richmond. I felt that I did not need the headache of pastoring any longer, and those that I had trusted betrayed me. One night as I was meditating, the Spirit of the Lord came to me and said, "What makes you so different than Jesus? If he experienced betrayal then suck it up and keep it moving." The Spirit of the Lord further reminded me that as he was with Jesus during his betrayal, so would he be with me. Now I know this may sound a little strange, but this is the very thing that kept me during this time of my life. I would also mention that there were those who were a part of the peanut gallery telling me I should just leave and go somewhere else. We always have to be mindful of those who try to rewrite our narrative in their effort to help. The individuals meant well, but this was my story, and if it was going to change, my orders would come from one person—the Lord himself.

After seeking the Lord further, I decided to enroll into seminary. Yes, the so-called *cemetery* that some would choose to think it was. Quite to the surprise of some, it was at the seminary that I really found Jesus! I found hope, I found help, and I found a whole lot of love! Sometimes when we are on the right path, it will lead us to places where others may not agree, but in the end, it will solidify our purpose and destiny.

For the next three years that I was a student at the seminary, I not only recovered my joy and love for ministry, but I met a host friends and colleagues that I'm still close with today. I do not blame or hold anything against my former leaders who discouraged me from going to seminary as I was growing up in the church. I'm just thankful I had enough courage to go and find out for myself. So many of us have been told by others what we should or should not do, simply because they did not do, but what I realized is that what you don't know will hurt you! We have to be wise enough to understand that some of the same people that don't want us to go places have some insecurities and are afraid that by us going, it will change us and our relationship with them. Ironically, the hope is that it will change us, but in a way that will make us better, not bitter; not distant from them but closer to the Lord.

## WE ARE CHANGE AGENTS

There was another occasion where I made one of those "I never" statements. I said, "I would never get involved in politics and run for office." Well, I had to eat those words as well. It was the third year of my pastorate, and several community leaders came to me and asked would I consider running for the board of supervisors. At the time, the county was in transition and there was need for major changes in the area. I struggled with the idea of running because I have always felt or was led to believe that politics and church don't mix. Now before you shoot me down, I still believe that they don't mix, but let me explain. There will always be politicians who have an agenda, and whoever supports their agenda is the side they will be on. However, I also believe if we are going to get God into government, we need godly people who are willing to be agents of change and then stand up for righteousness. Moreover, only praying about change and never getting involved in the process of change will never bring about change.

One of the greatest agents of change was Jesus Christ. He disrupted the status quo and made folks upset in the process. By our modern-day standards, Jesus was radical. He did not come to fit in but to bring about change. While I know this is and will always be a topic of debate, but for the sake of argument, Jesus was a politician. You may not agree, but the very definition of a politician is one who is active in government. He was not elected by the people but appointed by God. In fact, the prophet Isaiah mentioned that "the government shall be upon his shoulders" (Isaiah 9:6).

So, I ran for office. Although I lost by almost 200 votes, it was a tremendous learning experience. Not only did I meet many of the residents in the county, but I had the opportunity to hear their concerns. By running for office, I discovered that some people just want to be heard. A lot of times we are listening but not hearing their concerns. If we don't hear those who are affected by change, it serves no benefit. In the end we are all change agents, but if we don't get involved in the process by voting and registering individuals to vote, nothing will change. Although we may make certain statements early in life or in our careers as to what we will or won't do, never be afraid to admit that time brings about a change in all our lives. What we may have seen or said earlier sometimes changes after certain challenges and struggles in life.

**CHANGE COMES WHEN WE ARE WILLING TO CHANGE**
One of the last things that I said I would never do is to serve on any local boards. As an advocate of social change and racial diversity in local government, I always tend to speak my mind when it comes to certain issues. It's also my belief that if you are not going to make a difference and hold elected officials accountable, then it's no need to sit on a board or at the table just to say you are a board member.

Due to the lack of accountability and favoritism that was shown at times, I vowed to never serve on any local board. I know this was kind of a rash statement, but at the time I was disappointed with the way things were being handled. Well, I was asked to serve on another board outside of the county, but I declined. Fortunately, I was asked to serve again when a new group of elected officials came into office and this time I agreed to serve. So, what was the difference in me saying yes this time and no the first time? As strange as this may sound, sometimes our views change with time. Moreover, people have the tendency to change over time. The key, however, is not being afraid to say I see things differently now. Too many times we miss the opportunity to make a difference because we are locked into an old mindset but wanting to do a new thing. If we are ever going to change the status quo, it must begin with us.

Menspiration is about having the courage to say I was wrong and being bold enough to step up to accept the challenge of making a difference. By serving on the board, I was able to lead the way in bringing about a needed change for three counties. In addition, I was voted to serve as chair for three years. The remarkable thing about this entire process was if I had not agreed to serve on the board, many residents would not have benefited from the future decisions that were made by the board. Sometimes our pride gets in the way of progress and ultimately hinders what can be accomplished. We must never allow what we said we would never do in the past to hinder what needs to be done in the present. Holding on to past hurts and disappointments allow us to become slaves to our own mindset. Be bold enough to give yourself permission to change and in doing so, you open the door to greater possibilities for those whom you serve.

I learned so much about change as an educator, administrator, and government official. In these positions, a lot of what we do can become political if we allow local government officials to dictate what they think should be in the school versus what we know should be there. For example, due to the recent gun violence in our schools nationwide, local school officials are lobbying for more safety initiatives, such as more resource officers and more technology to alert school administration when there is an active shooter on campus. As a government official, it's not just our job to inform and educate, but to advocate change in the areas that can most impact our local community.

**TRUTH MOMENT**
To say the sky is the limit is an understatement to many now. In fact, with the number of satellites in space, that statement is almost obsolete. To say life is filled with many possibilities

and there are no limits is a more accurate statement. We have access to more now than we have ever had, and this suggests that the field is leveling off. Although the rules in certain circles have not changed, by and large we have made progress. To be able to complete the task of leaving something that will be around longer than us is not just about success but legacy. To finally be able to deliver something that's been kicking inside of you is a relief, and hopefully a blessing to others. To have been told as a fifteen-year-old young man that college was not in my DNA because neither my mother nor father went, was nothing but fuel for my journey. To be the first of six to not only finish college, but to receive a doctorate degree in education was fuel for my journey. To start a church in a rural southern community with the majority being college students was fuel for my journey. To coach a high school basketball team with some challenging young men and go to the state championship was fuel for my journey. To attend seminary after being told there were no benefits in going was fuel for my journey. To serve on a local governing board after saying I would never serve was fuel for my journey. To serve as Dean of Students at a high school that never had one was fuel for my journey. Finally, to write this book after years of trying is my hope that it will be fuel for your journey.

# A Final Word
*Mending and Blending a New Way of Life*

In life we all hope that when our time comes to give account of what was done in this body, it can at least be said that we did something or said something that may have changed the course of another person's life. *Menspiration* is more about mending and blending motivational and inspirational stories hoping to change the game for us all, no matter how we were raised. The truth is we are more alike than different. Too often we have been beat up and not built up, and consequently, we are reluctant to share our story. I have given you snap shots of my life hoping you will be able to identify similar struggles.

Earlier I shared the story of the gentleman who was on the seashore and took the time to throw as many starfish as he could back into the ocean hoping to save their lives. My question to you is this: who do you identify with in the story? Are you the person who looks at others and feels there is no need to throw the starfish back into the sea because there are too many and it takes too much time? Do you only have time for what you think is important, and will you go through life never taking any risk to change one person's life at the expense of many? Or are you that person who sees the importance in sacrificing your time, talent, or treasure to make a difference in another's life and perhaps saving it no matter what others may think or say? Finally, are you that person who lives his life not knowing if you are going to be rescued or saved by another person? Perhaps you were washed up on shore by the high tides (good times) or low tides (bad times) and are waiting for someone else to change the course of your life because your destiny is in their hand?

Wherever you find yourself currently, you must realize that you have choices in life and it is up to you to be intentional about your decisions regardless of what others may say. In doing so, your decision may be the inspiration for one or because you were intentional, it may be the motivation for another as they come along the way. At the end of the day, when you blend the two—motivation and inspiration—it equates to *Menspiration*. This is what changes the game. No longer do we have to blame our fathers for not being there because we still have a blueprint before us. Additionally, *Menspiration* is not about a perfect prescription for success, but rather a working manual that changes over time. It is what we call a living document; it is continually updated and revised. The hope is that we can all become Menspirations as we are updated and revised daily.

# Endnotes

## Chapter 2

1. Nick Saban, *How Good Do You Want to Be?: A Champion's Tips on How to Lead and Succeed at Work and in Life* (New York: Random House Publishing, 2005), 3-5.

2. Vince Lombardi, Jr., *What it Takes to be Number One* (New York: McGraw Hill, 2001), 125-127.

3. Rick Godwin, *Training for Reigning* (Lake Mary: Charisma House, 1997), 12-16

4. Frank Beamer, *Let Me be Frank: My Life at Virginia Tech* (California: Triumph Books, 2013), 12-14.

5. Edward L. Coles, *Maximize Manhood* (New Kensington: Whitaker Distribution, 1982), 35-37.

## Chapter 6

6. Myles Munroe, *Passing it On: Growing Future Leaders* ( New York: Hachette Book Group, 2011) 21-23.

7. Myles Munroe, *Passing it On: Growing Future Leaders* ( New York: Hachette Book Group, 2011) 158-159.

## Chapter 11

8. Myles Munroe, *Passing it On: Growing Future Leaders* ( New York: Hachette Book Group, 2011) 206-207.

# ABOUT THE AUTHOR

Dr. Ronald Thornhill, a native of Richmond, VA, is a devoted father, pastor, coach, educator, and author with a heart for God and man. He is known as the "Community's Pastor," as his powerful message of hope, healing, and liberation through Christ resonates among people from every walk of life and is propelling Southside, VA into a new realm.

He serves as the senior pastor of The Tabernacle of Zion Church in Lawrenceville, VA, a thriving ministry he founded 25 years ago. As part of his distinguished career, Dr. Thornhill serves as the Dean of Students and Athletic Director at Brunswick High School, chair of the Southside Community Services Board of Directors, and board member of the Southside Virginia Community College. He also hosts a daily radio broadcast that has inspired many over the years.

Dr. Thornhill's formal education includes a Bachelor's Degree in Business from Virginia Commonwealth University, a Master's Degree in Education from Old Dominion University, a Master's of Divinity from Virginia Union University, and a Doctorate Degree in Administration and Educational Leadership from Nova Southeastern University.

He is married to Patrice, who now co-pastors with him in ministry. To this union were born one daughter, Ashley, and one son, Ronald II. He also has one grandson, Joshua Josiah, who loves spending the summer with his grandfather.

For speaking engagements, conferences, book signings, and to add your location to the national book tour, contact:

Phone: 434.532.5228
Twitter: @drthornhill23
Facebook: menspirations

*Other Authors by*

**Fallen Chains**
*Samantha Campbell*
*ISBN ~ 978-0997992366*

**The Comeback**
*Darrin Williams*
*ISBN ~ 978-0997992328*

**Early Morning Visitor**
*Rolinda Butler*
*ISBN ~ 978-0997992304*

**The Love Between**
*Tiffany Hayes*
*ISBN ~ 978-0997992342*

**The Truth About the Facts**
*Dr. Chuck Wilson*
*ISBN ~ 978-0998831343*

**Daily Dose of Direction for Women in Business**
*Melanie Bonita*
*ISBN ~ 978-0998831305*